LITHUANIA
Facts and Figures

VILNIUS
Du Ka
1999

UDK 908 (474.5)
Li 578

ISBN 9986-647-09-6

CONTENTS

This land, which we inherited from our parents, belongs to us all. We call it Lithuania, and we make every effort to ensure that the name will never disappear. We write and pronounce it the same way that we articulate the names of other nations and states. We would like them to pronounce this name with the same respect.

JUSTINAS MARCINKEVIČIUS

THE LAND
AND ITS INHABITANTS

THE COUNTRY

Lithuania is located at the western end of the East European Plain, on the shores of the Baltic Sea.

In the north it borders Latvia (a 546km border); in the east and south, Belarus (650km); in the southwest, Poland (110km) and the Kaliningrad district of the Russian Federation (303km). Its land borders amount to a total of 1,609 kilometres. 99 kilometres of pristine Baltic Sea coastline form most of Lithuania's western border.

The country's northernmost point is at 56°27' and the southernmost one is at 53°54'. Its westernmost point is at 20°56' and its easternmost point is at 26°51'. In other words, Lithuania extends 373 kilometres from east to west, and 276 kilometres from north to south.

According to the French National Geographical Institute, the centre of Europe lies at 54°51' N and 25°19' E: that is, about 20 kilometres north of Vilnius. This point is marked by a commemorative stone.

Lithuania is in the Central European time zone (GMT + 1).

LANDSCAPE

Lithuania covers 65,300 square kilometres, making it larger than its neighbours, Latvia and Estonia, as well as Belgium, Denmark, the Netherlands and Switzerland.

The country's landscape is diverse, consisting of gently rolling plains (55% of the total land area), and extensive forests. The average height above sea level is 99 metres. The highest point is Juozapinė Hill (294m) in the Medininkai Plain of southeast Lithuania.

There are 758 rivers and streams longer than ten kilometres. The largest river in terms of volume is the Nemunas (total length 937km of which 475km flows through Lithuania). The incline of Lithuanian rivers is generally gradual, and their velocity is relatively low.

Lithuania boasts 2,830 lakes that are larger than 0.5 hectares. They cover 1.5% of the total land area (about 880 sq km). The high-

THE CURONIAN PENINSULA

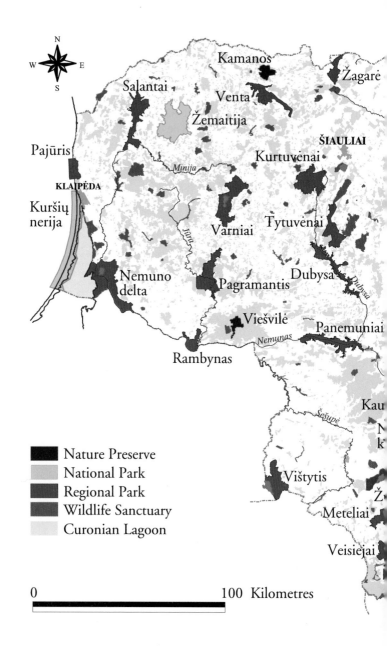

Nature Preserve
National Park
Regional Park
Wildlife Sanctuary
Curonian Lagoon

0   100   Kilometres

Protected Areas

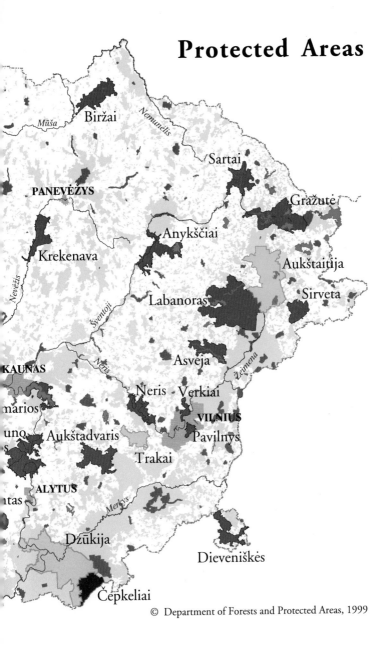

Müša
Biržai
Nemunėlis
Sartai
PANEVĖŽYS
Gražutė
Anykščiai
Krekenava
Aukštaitija
Nevėžis
Sirveta
Labanoras
Šventoji
Neris
Asveja
KAUNAS
Žeimena
Neris
Verkiai
marios
VILNIUS
uno
Aukštadvaris
Pavilnys
Trakai
ALYTUS
Merkys
tas
Dieveniškės
Dzūkija
Čepkeliai

A CORNER OF THE AUKSTAITIJA REGION

est concentration of lakes is in the eastern part of the country, including the largest, Drūkšiai (4,480ha), the longest, Asveja (21.9km), and the deepest, Tauragnas (60.5m).

The largest inland body of water, the *Kuršių marios* (Curonian Lagoon), is adjacent to the *Kuršių nerija* (Curonian Peninsula). The lagoon and peninsula were formed 5,000 years ago by the churning waves of the restless Baltic. The northern half of the lagoon (413 sq km) belongs to Lithuania; the southern part is in the Russian Kaliningrad district. Altogether, 25 rivers and streams flow into the *Kuršių marios*.

The Curonian Peninsula separating the Curonian Lagoon from the Baltic Sea is a remarkable natural phenomenon. The 50-kilometre-long Lithuanian portion of the peninsula is as narrow as 0.4 kilometres in some sections. Now a national park, the *Kuršių nerija* is an ecological treasure, and serves as an important resting spot for approximately 15 million birds during their annual migrations. Three elements prevail here: water, sand and wind. In the 18th century and later, whole areas of primeval forest were cut down, thereby exposing the thin soil to the battering winds rolling in from the Baltic. Eventually sandstorms and shifting dunes buried more than ten Curonian fishing villages.

Despite the winds, the *Kuršių nerija* receives the most sunshine year round of all other locations in Lithuania.

A total of 1.88 million hectares of the country (30.3%) is covered by forests. Pine and fir trees dominate. More than 53% of Lithuanian forests are still owned by the state, which operates an extensive forest management service, although private ownership of forest land is on the increase. The most extensive forest stands are in the Alytus and Vilnius counties in the south and the southeast.

As for the amount of wood per hectare, Lithuanian forests (at 186 cu m/ha) exceed the totals of the forests of Finland, Norway, Great Britain, Sweden, Denmark, Belarus and Latvia. Lithuania possesses over 347 million cubic metres of timber resources.

Over 734,000 hectares of Lithuania's natural heritage is under protection. Lithuanians take pride in their unspoiled natural landscape and have gone to great lengths to preserve its beauty for future generations. There are four nature reserves, 30 regional parks, and about 750 protected landscape objects.

The protected areas encompass 334,100 hectares, or 16.9% of the country's total forest area.

NATIONAL PARKS

The first national parks were established some two decades ago to preserve the most aesthetic natural features of the Lithuanian landscape, wildlife habitats and places of ethnographic interest. At the same time, Lithuania's national parks are a focal point for recreation, ranging from one-day outings to natural history tours and ecological tourism.

In the south the national parks protect the bulk of the best forest land; in the northeast they guard the natural beauty of upland lakes. Each park also preserves valuable reminders of the local heritage, including farm buildings, agricultural implements and folk sculptures.

The national parks are excellent places for relaxation, fishing and sightseeing. Increasingly, traditional village houses are being fitted out to accommodate tourists. Boats for hire, information and other services are generally readily available. The parks are inhabited by game not often found in Western Europe, such as elk and wolves. Deer and wild boar are common throughout the country's uninhabited areas.

Aukštaitija National Park

In northeast Lithuania, the Aukštaitija National Park (established in 1974) is characterised by gently rolling hills and sparkling lakes and streams. The park is studded with 102 lakes of varying size, many of which can be seen at a glance from almost any hill. From Ladakalnis Hill, the visitor can take in a spectacular panorama of six lakes surrounded by the dark greenery of pine, fir and oak trees. Forests cover 60% of the park's total area. Small lakeside resorts are used for summer tourism. The lakes of the Aukštaitija National Park are connected by 34 rivers and streams, thus offering excellent opportunities for canoeing. A complete tour through the park's lakes would take about a week.

Motorists can drive to the nearby Museum of Beekeeping, and visit two picturesque water mills that have survived from the past. Visitors may purchase a fishing licence and try their luck.

Kuršių Nerija National Park

The *Kuršių nerija* (Curonian Peninsula) National Park was formally established only in 1991, although its delicate landscape was protected from human exploitation in the pre-war period. The Curonian Peninsula, with its towering dunes - some of which still shift with the wind - its wide beaches and lush wood, attracts visitors from around the world. Almost all the woods that a contemporary might see were planted by local residents to stop the sand from shifting. At present, the Kuršių Nerija National Park includes the settlements of Juodkrantė, Pervalka, Preila and Nida. These former fishing villages have modern accommodation and are well equipped for tourism.

They are linked by the road from Klaipėda to Kaliningrad, or can be reached by yacht and motorboat. Tourists enjoy the extensive network of cycling routes; the over 50 kilometres of sandy beaches are open to swimmers and beachcombers.

Virtually all of the coast along the Lithuanian side of the peninsula is unspoiled (most construction is prohibited), and even in the summer, a visitor can enjoy long stretches of beach almost all to himself. The well-maintained traditional architecture complements the natural features of this nature preserve. The park is home to some rare, protected flora as well as elks, deer, fox and sea birds. Most first-time visitors are pleasantly surprised and decide to return.

Žemaitija National Park

The Žemaitija National Park is just 45 kilometres from the Baltic Sea, and can be reached easily from Klaipėda or Palanga. The Žemaičiai uplands are centred around Lake Plateliai, the pride of the park. This, as well as the other 26 lakes in this nature preserve, are beloved by locals and visitors from more distant locations in Lithuania. Lake Plateliai has seven islands.

This part of the region is famous for the town of Žemaičių Kalvarija, with its 19 chapels scattered over 12 hills. They were built in the 17th century, and today important religious festivals are often celebrated here. The park has 222 protected edifices, mainly small chapels and wooden sculptures.

Dzūkija National Park

Dzūkija National Park is in southern Lithuania, and evergreen forests occupy over 60% of it. The sandy soil is not favourable for agriculture, and therefore the locals traditionally have found work in forestry. Local residents are fond of gathering berries, mushrooms and wild honey. The ethnographic villages in the national park are scattered among the pine forests, and are characterised by their unusual architecture, their wooden houses, and large

13

yards. They are surrounded by relatively small fields, and, beyond them, the forests. The park has two larger rivers, suitable for canoeing, and quite a few smaller ones, which are a marvel to explore. One of them, the Skroblus, is notable for its meandering

course and high, vertical, sandy banks. The roads are good and offer easy access to all objects of interest. The park is an easy two-hour drive from Vilnius.

Trakai National Historical Park

This park is located about 30 kilometres from Vilnius. It is

DZŪKIJA NATIONAL PARK

dotted with 33 lakes, which determined the siting there of the old town of Trakai and its imposing castle. Especially interesting is Lake Galvė with its 21 islands. On one of them stands a major symbol of Lithuania's statehood, the castle of Vytautas Magnus, with its red brick towers looking out over the placid waters of the lake. Trakai contains numerous archaeological and historical monuments; it has been shaped by history and by the fact that the town traditionally was cohabited by numerous ethnic groups.

WILDLIFE

Lithuania's natural areas are home to numerous species of wildlife, some of which are otherwise quite rare. In 1999 the Ministry of the Environment published the following wildlife population data:

Elk (Moose, *Am*) - 4,850

Wolves – 480

Bison – 45

Beavers – 31,750

Deer – 15,430

Grey hares – 77,000

Wild boar – 23,000

Roe deer – 54,200

Fallow deer – 460

Foxes – 23,300

Woodgrouse – 500

Cranes – 800 pairs

Black storks – 700 pairs

THE WHITE STORK

There is a saying that you will meet kind people on a farm which has a nest with storks in it. For centuries storks in Lithuania have

TRAKAI HISTORICAL NATIONAL PARK, LOCATED 30KM SOUTHWEST
OF VILNIUS

been regarded as a link between man and nature, and therefore in folklore the stork is a spiritual, sacred bird. Thus it is only natural that in 1973 the white stork was proclaimed the national bird of Lithuania.

Counts carried out in many European countries show that there are 130,000 pairs of storks in Europe. Twelve thousand pairs (8.4% of all pairs of European storks) live in Lithuania, which is the highest density on the continent (17.6 pairs per 100 sq km).

Throughout Europe the stork population is diminishing. In Germany and France they are protected as birds threatened with extinction.

The loss of natural habitat, which resulted from reclamation of land and excessive use of chemicals in agriculture during the Soviet era, reduced the stork population in Lithuania. But during the past few years their population has reached and even surpassed previous levels. The more food there is, as in the flood plains of the lower Nemunas, the more storks' nests there will be. Over 1,000 stork pairs nest in the Šilutė district of western Lithuania,

making it one of the most densely inhabited stork nesting areas in Europe.

NATURAL RESOURCES

Lithuania is not well known for the abundance of its underground resources. The ground contains limestone, clay, sand, dolomite, peat, mineral water and some crude oil. Swedish and Danish oil producing firms have been co-operating with Lithuanian oil experts in prospecting for and drilling in the western districts of the country. Over 200,000 tons of high-grade oil are produced annually, and this total is expected to rise in the coming years.

Offshore oil resources are thought to be at least as large as onshore fields. A considerable amount of iron ore has been found in the southeastern part of Lithuania near the town of Varėna, triggering discussion between environmentalists and proponents of business development as to the wisdom of exploiting this resource.

An experimental geothermal project is close to completion near the port city of Klaipėda. Once completed it will satisfy a major part of the city's hot water demand in the summer.

Generation of hydroelectric power from small river dams is making a modest comeback. Several small projects have been going on stream each year. The largest hydroelectric power project in service is on the Nemunas near Kaunas.

CLIMATE

Lithuania's climate is part continental. The prevailing western winds bring warm humid air from the Baltic Sea. The average annual temperature is 6.2°C. Winters are moderately cold and summers comfortable. The warmest month is July, with daytime temperatures averaging in the low 20s, and the coldest is January (-5.1°C). Periodic warm fronts occasionally bring summer temperatures up to 30°C. The coldest recorded temperatures, usually in the southeast corner of the country, have been in the low 20s. The eastern side of the Curonian Peninsula (Nida) is the warmest part of the country.

The highest level of precipitation is in the southwestern part of the Žemaitija Plain (up to 930mm), the lowest in the north (about 550mm). The growing season lasts from 169 to 202 days.

LITHUANIA'S REGIONS

There are four main regions in Lithuania, commonly called ethnographic regions. This is because each one has a distinct character expressed by differences in its folk culture. They also differ in their topography, flora and fauna, and each one has its own dialect version of the language.

Aukštaitija

The largest region covers the north, east and middle of the country. Its name comes from the word *aukštai,* meaning high, as it includes a range of hilly uplands.

Aukštaitija is a land of pristine forests and beautiful lakes, and is immensely popular with tourists during the summer months. Despite this, it has managed to retain its unspoilt charm. The country's deepest (Tauragnas) and its largest lake (Drūkšiai) can be found here. Many of the forests are very old and some have never heard the sound of an axe felling a tree. The famous oak tree at Stelmužė is thought to be 1,500 years old.

The region has a pronounced rural character. Farms here are generally small, as it was customary among farmers to divide their land between their sons. There are many villages designated as ethnographic, in which an older, quieter way of life has been preserved. There is a wide variety of museums of local folklore and farming, among them a beekeeping museum in the village of Stripeikiai. Among the many towns of interest is Anykščiai, the home town of a number of popular writers. The region is also renowned for its beer and is home to two of Lithuania's largest breweries, in Utena and Panevėžys, as well as many smaller ones.

Dzūkija

The southern region of the country sits astride the Nemunas and borders Poland and Belarus. Most of it is forested. The name comes from a quirk of the dialect: people here often put the letter z after a consonant.

Dzūkijans are characterised by their optimism and their love of songs, and are known for having preserved many older traditions. This is a popular area for picking mushrooms in the summer and autumn, when not only Dzūkijans but also people from other parts of the country come out in search of these mysterious fungi.

Culinary specialities include, naturally, mushroom dishes and also many dishes made with potatoes and buckwheat.

Among the region's towns is the old health resort of Druskininkai. The region is full of curiosities related to woodland cul-

THE LAND AND ITS INHABITANTS

ture, including a number of botanical reserves and ancient villages closely connected to the life of the forest.

Suvalkija

The smallest region takes its name from the town of Suvalkai, now in Poland. This area has also been known in the past as Užnemunė (The Other Side of the Nemunas).

The countryside here is flat and covered with small farmsteads circled by trees. The region has always been a major agricultural producer.

Suvalkijans are renowned for their efficiency, pragmatism, love of order, and occasionally a touch of miserliness.

The area produces a famous kind of smoked sausage, called *skilandis,* which is filled with minced, seasoned meat.

Žemaitija

The westernmost region (historically called Samogitia) was first mentioned in records in the 13th century. The people here are well known for their industriousness. A large number of jokes also testifies to their stubbornness.

The traditional capital of the region, Telšiai, is a pleasant, quiet town situated on the edge of a lake. The Alka Museum in the town records the archaeology, history, flora and fauna of the area and of the country as a whole. It also holds a rare and impressive collection of Lithuanian and Western European art.

There are other museums in the region, covering folklore, rural life, various local writers and artists, and a museum dedicated to the culture of former country estates.

The lake at Plateliai lies at the heart of a national park and is very popular in summer.

Žemaitija is well known for its dairy produce. The region is also famous for the Žemaitukai horse, short but strong and energetic. A few years ago it was close to extinction, but now its numbers are increasing again.

People from Žemaitija are notoriously slow to accept change, but once they accept it, they embrace it fully. Žemaitijan pagans were the last people in Europe to accept Christianity.

NATIONAL DISHES

Traditionally, during a meal, the table would be covered with a linen tablecloth. Bread was put on the table at the very beginning, for it was considered sacred. A loaf of bread could never be placed on the table upside down, as this was considered disrespectful. A consecrated piece of bread used to be put into the foundations of a new building or carried by travellers during a journey.

Lithuania is relatively small; however, the cuisine of the various regions differs. Samogitians (*žemaičiai*) eat porridge, stew and *kastinis* (similar to cottage cheese). Aukštaitijans enjoy various pancake and curd dishes. Dzūkijans are very fond of buckwheat, which grows well in their sandy soil; they are also skilled in collecting and drying mushrooms and preserving them in other ways. Suvalkijans enjoy smoked meat, especially pork.

The oldest Lithuanian foodstuff is rye grain for making rye bread. Some of the most popular kinds of rye bread can be found in any food shop in Lithuania, and include *Bočiai, Palanga, Rugelis, Dzūkų* and *Pajūris*. Vilnius bakeries produce 15 kinds of rye bread. Some varieties are baked with nuts, raisins, whole grains, caraway and sunflower seeds, while others are even baked over marsh reeds. Some rye breads are noted for their coarse texture and partially milled rye grains, while others leave a pleasant sour taste. Over 70% of the bread consumed in Lithuania is dark, rye bread.

Pork is the most popular meat, and it is eaten fresh, salted or smoked. Lithuanians also make a great variety of sausages.

Šaltibarščiai, cold beet soup, is a favourite dish on hot summer days. Served with sour cream and an accent of dill, with hot potatoes on the side, it makes for a delicious meal in itself.

Potatoes are of great importance in the national cuisine, and potato pancakes covered with bacon or sour cream are universal favourites. Potatoes only appeared in the 18th century, but as early as the first half of the next century, they had become as important as bread for the common people.

Lithuania is a beer-loving country. Today, most beer is produced in large, modern breweries, though in the north, home-made beer is also brewed. For family celebrations or major holidays, home-made beer is sometimes brewed by the householder himself.

POPULATION DATA

Lithuania's population totals 3.7 million people, of which 68.2% live in urban areas. Women constitute 52.8% of the population. Their average lifespan is 76.8 years, ten years more than the average man's. Since 1994 natural reproduction has been decreasing due to the declining birth rate; also, emigration has been higher than immigration. According to the last census (1989), the average size of a family was 3.2 people. Only one per cent of families had ten or more members. In all, 81.6% of the population are ethnic Lithuanians.

In the past, the country's population was decimated by wars, and after serfdom was abolished in 1861, there was a mass emigration. From 1861 to 1914, almost 700,000 people emigrated, mainly to the United States. From 1915 to 1940 Latin America became the chief destination for thousands more emigrants. Another 60,000 people, many well educated, fled from the advancing Russian armies in 1944. Most of the latter wound up in the United States, Canada and Australia. Mass deportations also significantly reduced the population between 1941 and 1953.

At present about one million Lithuanians live abroad. According to the 1980 census, 743,000 of these live in the USA. The other large communities are in Canada, Australia, Brazil, Argentina, Uruguay, Great Britain, Germany, Poland and Latvia.

ETHNIC MINORITIES

Lithuania is inhabited by people of 109 different ethnic backgrounds. The most numerous ethnic groups are Russians (304,800,

POPULATION DYNAMICS AND DENSITY			
Year	Population	Urban Population	Density (per sq km)
1400	260,000	–	4.0
1528	330,000	–	5.0
1569	420,000	–	6.4
1650	960,000	–	14.7
1790	990,000	12.4%	15.2
1857	1,910,000	–	29.3
1897	2,673,000	13.3%	41.0
1914	2,828,000	13.0%	43.4
1923	2,620,000	17.7%	40.2
1940	3,084,000	21.9%	47.3
1950	2,573,000	28.3%	39.5
1959	2,711,000	38.6%	41.6
1965	2,954,000	43.9%	45.3
1970	3,128,000	50.2%	48.0
1975	3,295,000	56.3%	50.5
1979	3,398,000	60.7%	52.1
1985	3,570,000	65.7%	54.8
1990	3,708,000	68.1%	56.8
1999	3,700,000	68.1%	56.7

or 8.2% of the total population), Poles (256,600, or 6.9%), Belarusians (54,500, or 1.5%), Ukrainians (36,900, or 1%), Jews (5,200, 0.1%), and others (24,900, 0.7%). Most inhabitants from a non-Lithuanian background live in east and southeast Lithuania, Vilnius, Klaipėda and Visaginas (in the northeast).

According to the 1989 Law on Ethnic Minorities (amended in 1991), all citizens of the Republic of Lithuania, regardless of their ethnic background, are guaranteed equal political, economic and social rights. The law guarantees minorities' cultural integrity, promotes their national consciousness and its expression. The Nationalities Department was established to deal with the specific needs of minority communities; later it was renamed the Department of National Minorities and Lithuanians Living Abroad. Both this law and this Government institution are the first of their kind in Eastern and Central Europe.

Constitutional Rights

The Constitution of the Republic of Lithuania guarantees citizens belonging to ethnic minorities the right to cultivate their native language, culture and traditions. Every person has the right to choose any religion or faith and, either individually or with others, express his or her religion through worship, observance, practice or the instruction of children. The rights of ethnic minorities are also regulated by bilateral agreements with Russia, Belarus, Poland and Ukraine, as well as by international agreements.

Affirmative State Support

Lithuania devotes a great deal of care and considerable resources to bilingual education. There are 226 secondary schools in which the language of instruction is either Russian, Polish, or another non-Lithuanian language. These schools are attended by 67,546 pupils, which amounts to 12.8% of the country's school-age children. Some ethnic minority communities organise Sunday schools.

There are 56 periodicals published in languages other than Lithuanian, including 43 in Russian, seven in Polish, four in German and one in Belarusian. The Jewish community publishes a newspaper in four languages. The Greek and Tartar communities have periodicals in Lithuanian and Russian, with sections in their native languages.

Lithuanian national radio and TV stations regularly broadcast programmes in Russian, Polish, Ukrainian and Belarusian. Programmes are also broadcast for the Jewish community. Since 1992 a private Polish radio station, *Znad Wilii,* has been broadcasting 24 hours a day on two frequencies. A Russian broadcasting station, Radio 7, has been operating since autumn 1997.

Over 200 public organisations have been established by the members of 19 ethnic minorities. Government funding supports a variety of cultural endeavours by the minority communities. About 100 ethnic folk groups exist in Lithuania. The Russian and Polish communities have political organisations of their own, and participate in elections to the Seimas. The Polish Electoral Action Party has two seats in the Seimas, and holds a majority in two local administrations.

THE LANGUAGE

Lithuanian, and the kindred Latvian, belong to the Baltic group of Indo-European languages. Lithuanian and Latvian are thought to have separated from a common stem some time in the seventh century. Lithuanian, among all of the living Indo-European languages, has been the most successful in preserving its ancient system of phonetics and most of its morphological features. The alphabet consists of 32 letters. Lithuanian has 59 phonemes, 11 parts of speech, two genders, seven cases, two aspects, two voices, five moods, four tenses, three persons. The order of words in the sentence is quite free, mainly subject to style. The orthography is morphological; however, phonology is also taken into account. The language has two major dialects: *aukštaičių* (highlander) and *žemaičių* (lowlander). Linguists divide them into numerous sub-dialects, which are still spoken.

The written language evolved relatively late, on account of such historical factors as the late adoption of Christianity. The history of the written language starts in Lithuania Minor (East Prussia) in the middle of the 16th century. The very first book written in Lithuanian was *Catechismus* by Martynas Mažvydas, published in 1547.

Although writing in the 16th and 17th centuries was dominated by an ecclesiastical style, which was somewhat distant from the style employed by the common people, it grew and consolidated. Of great importance was Mikalojus Daukša's *Postilė* (1599)

POSTILĖ (1599) BY MIKALOJUS DAUKŠA: ONE OF THE FIRST BOOKS TO BE PUBLISHED IN THE GRAND DUCHY OF LITHUANIA

25

and Konstantinas Sirvydas' tri-lingual (Polish-Latin-Lithuanian) dictionary (circa 1620). The latter represented a milestone in the codification of written Lithuanian. In addition, a Lithuanian grammar by Danielius Kleinas was published in 1653.

Rise of Polish Influence

From the beginning of the 18th century, the role of written Lithuanian in the Grand Duchy of Lithuania declined, as most Catholic priests and writers distanced themselves from the people and adopted the socially more prestigious Polish culture. During this period, an important volume was an anonymous grammar (1737), which was the first work to describe Lithuanian accents.

Although the role of the language was declining in the Grand Duchy, the opposite tendency was apparent in Lithuania Minor. In the 1760s, Kristijonas Donelaitis wrote *The Seasons,* a poem giving expression to the common people's rich spoken traditions. The influence of Donelaitis on Lithuanian literature is comparable to that of Dante on Italian, or Shakespeare on English.

The 19th century was not a very favourable time for the development of the Lithuanian lan-guage: most of the country was occupied by Russia, a smaller part by Prussia. However, as the study of comparative linguistics emerged, the language attracted increasing attention because of its archaic features. This interest gave rise to a new wave of Lithuanian grammars. August Schleicher, a German linguist with a special interest in the history of Indo-European languages, published his famous *Litauische Grammatik* in 1856; it was the first Lithuanian grammar written by applying the comparative-historical method. The most detailed and complete grammar was published by Frydrichas Kuršaitis in 1876.

Tsarist Prohibition of the Latin Script

After 1864, when the use of the Roman alphabet was prohibited by the Tsarist regime, books and papers written in the forbidden alphabet continued to be printed in East Prussia and the USA, and smuggled across the border. About 1,450 publications were thus printed and disseminated during the prohibition. During this period, the language was extensively researched by leading linguists of the time, such as Filip Fortunatov, Jan Baudouin de Courtenay, August Leskien and Ferdinand de Saussure.

Modern Lithuanian Established

It was only at the beginning of the 20th century that the current alphabet came into general use. In the Grand Duchy of Lithuania, Gothic letters were commonly employed until the 18th century. The Gothic form of writing survived in Lithuania Minor until the beginning of the Second World War.

The works of the linguists Jonas Jablonskis and Kazimieras Būga are of special importance to the codification of Lithuanian. The orthography that Jablonskis employed in his *Grammar* in 1922 has been in use up to the present without any substantial changes.

After independence was reestablished, one of the most pressing needs was the rationalisation of orthography and the codification of specific terms. Leading writers of the time contributed to the codification of the written language.

During the 1950s and 1960s, Vilnius became the leading centre for research into Lithuanian, and the Baltic languages, while departments of Lithuanian or Baltic Studies were established in many universities around the world. Especially important have been the works of leading foreign Baltists such as Ernst Frenkel (Germany), Christian Stang (Norway) and Jan Otrębski (Poland).

Since 1954, specialised dictionaries have been published. So far, the first 18 volumes of a projected 20-volume Lithuanian dictionary have been published. Research for this massive undertaking is based on 4.5 million entries on Lithuanian words maintained at the Institute of the Lithuanian Language.

In 1988, as the movement for Lithuanian freedom was gaining momentum, Lithuanian was proclaimed the state language. This move was in response to popular concern about the inroads that Russian was making in administration, employment, education and the media at the time. Subsequently, in 1995, the Law on the State Language was passed to specify the role of Lithuanian in public life and the means of teaching the language to non-native speakers.

THE OLD TOWN OF VILNIUS

CITIES

The capital of Lithuania
pop. 578,400

Jan Bulhak, a distinguished photographer who worked in Vilnius, remarked: "Vilnius is a state of spirit lightened by sun rays." This spirituality is perhaps the strongest quality of the city. It became the capital in the 14th century and is the centre for Lithuanian history and culture.

The Historical and Cultural Heritage

Vilnius is frequently referred to as the city of Gediminas, the Grand Duke of Lithuania. Indeed, it was he who established it as the capital of the Lithuanian state.

The city flourished in the 16th century. An academy (now Vilnius University) was established in 1579, and books were printed there in Lithuanian, Polish, Old Slavonic and other languages. Vilnius became one of the centres for religious and secular culture in Central and Eastern Europe. It attracted people of various cultures, and became famous for its scientists and artists.

The main feature of the city is the symbiosis of cultures. From the 14th century, the Grand Duchy of Lithuania was a multi-ethnic state. It was famous in Europe for its religious tolerance. This policy was started by Grand Duke Gediminas. In 1323 he invited to his capital tradesmen, craftsmen, and monks and priests, promising that Christians, as well as people of other faiths, would be permitted to practise their religion. Later, other peoples settled in Vilnius. Grand Duke Vytautas invited

29

Crimean Tartars and Karaites at the beginning of the 15th century. Fortified Tartar settlements were a part of the defence system of the city and its environs. Vilnius was also important for Belarusian and Ukrainian culture: in the 16th century the first books in Belarusian were printed here.

THE GOTHIC ST ANNE'S CHURCH, BUILT AT THE END OF THE 15TH CENTURY

Jewish Settlement

From the 15th century, Jews moved to Lithuania, leaving Western Europe due to persecution. Gradually the capital became a multicultural city and a centre for numerous faiths. Ethnic and religious groups established communities, had a degree of legal autonomy, and erected houses of worship. Jews referred to Vilnius as the Jerusalem of

Lithuania (Yerushalaiyme de Lita). By the 16th century, the city had become a leading centre for Jewish learning. Before the Second World War, Vilnius had 96 synagogues.

Architecture

Vilnius mixes the work of man and nature: its architecture follows natural forms and emphasises them, whereas nature frames the architecture and mingles with the city's spaces. By the 15th century, travellers had begun to notice the exceptional natural charm of the capital of the Grand Duchy of Lithuania and its architecture. In a relatively small area, a landscape of plains and hills was formed. Two deep valleys are carved out by the two rivers, the Neris and the Vilnia, very different in their size and character. From ancient times to the Second World War, the Neris was an important waterway. On its banks stood elegant palaces belonging to nobles and bishops, and richly decorated monasteries with charming Baroque churches.

In the oldest part of the city, where the remains of the castles are, the Neris is joined by the short (only 90km in length) but rapid Vilnia. It is this stream which gave its name to Vilnius.

Flanked by these valleys and hills (from three sides, except the north), as if in the middle of a giant pot, the city of Vilnius grew up. These surroundings contribute to the city's charm. Only in the 20th century did it step outside this hollow, and now it is expanding beyond the hills.

The hills offer an excellent panorama of the city. The view of old Vilnius, with its labyrinth of narrow streets, churches and bell towers, red tile roofs and a multitude of trees, can be appreciated best from the top of Gediminas Hill which, like a monolith created by the Neris and Vilnia, occupies the heart of the city.

In terms of architecture, the central part of Vilnius is the richest. It consists of two main parts: the Old Town (Senamiestis) and the New Town (Naujamiestis).

The New Town started forming in the 19th century, and is interesting for its Historicism and 20th-century architecture. Major government institutions, the parliament, city council and most ministries, can be found there, as well as banks, theatres and upmarket shops. It also has the capital's main street, *Gedimino prospektas*, which extends almost two kilometres.

The Old Town is the heart of the capital, the oldest and

31

THE GATES OF DAWN STREET 1846. LITHOGRAPH BY ALPHONSE BICHEBOIS AND VICTOR ADAM. FROM A DRAWING BY KAROL RIPINSKI AND MARTIN ZALESKI

THE GATES OF DAWN STREET TODAY

architecturally the richest part of Vilnius. It is one of the largest old town centres in Central and Eastern Europe, covering almost 360 hectares and including over 1,500 buildings. Almost every style of architecture can be found: from Gothic to Post-Modernism. Due to its historical and architectural value, the Old Town was declared a World Heritage Site by UNESCO in 1994.

RŪDNINKŲ STREET AT NIGHT

Vilnius was born from its castles, and these are among the country's most important historical sites. The area taken up by the castles occupies almost 80 hectares. In the Middle Ages, it consisted of three castles: the Upper (on Gediminas Hill), the Lower (at the foot of the hill), and the Crooked Castle (on the opposite bank of the Vilnia). Today, only the ruins of the Upper Castle and Gediminas Tower survive (the latter offers a splendid view of the city). Also, parts of the Lower Castle remain, including the most important of them, the Cathedral, first built in the 13th century and then subject to numerous alterations. This important piece of 18th-century Classical architecture (by the architect Laurynas Stuoka-Gucevičius) has survived to our day. The Crooked Castle did not survive, and only pleasant woods and Three Crosses Hill mark its location. In 1997, the parliament conferred on the castle area the status of a national cultural reservation.

Vilnius has preserved up to now its old network of streets. It is characterised by the irregular lines of streets, small squares and streets widening at their convergence. The city started forming in pagan times, when it consisted of a few separate settlements. The network changed only once, at the turn of the 15th and 16th centuries, when the defence system changed and a city wall was erected. In subsequent centuries, Vilnius became denser. It avoided the dramatic changes in the 17th and

18th centuries characteristic of major European cities, and in the 19th century it expanded into the present-day Naujamiestis. In this way, Vilnius preserved its ancient features. The streets generally belong to two types. The first, the oldest type, included trade roads. They are relatively wide and straight, quite long, with graceful buildings of serious architectural quality, mainly palaces. The lanes are quite different: they are crooked, and often forced their buildings into their shape.

Since old Vilnius is constructed on hills, it is rich in its pattern of streets. Anyone who raises his eyes above the narrow streets will see a variety of roofs, as if from a Cézanne painting, the towers and cupolas of distant churches, the tops of trees growing in courtyards, and the green hills surrounding the city.

Churches are the pride of Vilnius, offering a wide architectural diversity. In terms of architecture, Vilnius is a city of churches. Almost all of them have survived up to this day. Their distribution around the city is far from typical. The Cathedral was erected not in a major square but in the castle precinct; its surrounding square was completed only in 1940. Other churches are not distributed evenly across the city but tend to group themselves in twos, threes or fours, sometimes even bringing together different religions and denominations.

The architectural styles of the churches are especially unusual and interesting. Lithuania does not have soft stone, therefore, the Gothic churches were built from bricks, moulded in about 150 patterns. Out of these pieces, craftsmen constructed complex edifices, with star and crystal vaults. St Anne's Church is perhaps the best example of this style. Other Gothic churches exist, with thick

SUMMERTIME IN THE OLD TOWN

walls like fortifications. Their facades are decorated by blind niches, and patterns with symbolic meanings rooted in pagan times. The interiors of the churches have complex vaults and wall paintings.

The pride of Vilnius church architecture is its Baroque, which has been well preserved. A masterpiece of 17th-century Baroque is St Peter and Paul's Church, located in the suburb of Antakalnis. Its interior is covered with stucco figures and patterns. St Peter and Paul's Church is an enormous theatre of sculptures: on every surface, the nave, the pulpit, the walls and ceilings of the chapels, are figures, about 3,000 in total, which narrate stories, explain the Christian faith, illustrate the theology of St Augustine, and teach us about the history of the Pacas family, the nobles who founded the church.

According to Bulhak, in the 19th century, every day one met visitors for whom Vilnius was an unexpected discovery, a deeply moving experience. This atmosphere is maintained by the modern capital, the country's largest city, with 578,400 inhabitants.

Vilnius Today
In 1998 and 1999 major renovation and resoration work in the Old Town was undertaken, which already has attracted favourable comment from visitors and foreign journalists.

Modern Vilnius is a bustling city, which is becoming a showcase for Lithuania's economic achievements since the restoration of independence. Visitors who return after an absence of a year or two are nearly universally impressed with the pace of visible change. Indeed, in some respects, the Vilnius of 1990 and the capital of today are two different cities.

One very visible change is the traffic. If in 1990 Vilnius seemed only on the verge of mass automobile ownership, with one (generally Russian-made) car for seven to eight city residents, today this ratio is something like one private car for every two inhabitants. Over a quarter of a million cars make rush hour in Vilnius as complicated as it is in most comparably sized Western European cities. Parking in 1991 was almost never a problem (one could park one's car in front of the opera building ten minutes before the start of a premiere). Now, however, the choicest spots in the Old Town and commercial centre are designated paid parking areas. Nevertheless, prices are still very reasonable – the equivalent of two US dollars per day.

Most of the world's major car manufacturers have authorised dealerships and, increasingly, modern service stations for the growing numbers of sophisticated car buyers. Shell, Statoil, Neste and Texaco petrol stations feature convenience stores, auto accessories and car washes.

Private shopping centres, supermarkets and boutiques have almost completely replaced the old state-owned shops, with their scanty selection and indifferent service.

Vilnius had only one private restaurant in late 1991, but this number has climbed into the hundreds and now includes a cosmopolitan offering of cuisines typical of Western cities. The more affluent Vilnius residents and foreign visitors can now pick and choose among Chinese, Japanese, Indian, Malay, Mexican, Georgian, Russian, Italian and US-style restaurants, and this list is far from complete.

Hotel accommodation has taken a giant leap forward, with

the opening of some 30 new, mostly modest-sized private hotels and inns in the last few years. Vilnius' first business-class hotel, the Radisson SAS Astorija, opened its doors only in 1998 and is already undergoing major expansion.

Nearly 20 private art galleries and numerous antique shops provide visitors with plenty of opportunities to browse and shop. During the concert season, Vilnius residents and guests have a truly rich selection of offerings. Often on any fall or winter evening, as many as three or four major musical performances are held simultaneously, including opera, symphony or chamber orchestra music and solo recitals.

VILNIUS NOW HAS AN EXTENSIVE NETWORK OF MODERN DEPARTMENT STORES

KAUNAS

KAUNAS

Pop. 414,200

Distance from Vilnius – 102km

If one were to imagine Kaunas in the past one might conjure up the medieval Knights of the Cross besieging the fortress of Kaunas at the junction of the Neris and the Nemunas rivers. A place of strategic importance, Kaunas was a tempting target for the Crusaders rampaging on Lithuanian soil. For this reason, the fall of the Kaunas fortress in 1361 (this is the date the city first appears in chronicles) was a great defeat for Lithuanians in their struggles against the invading Teutonic Order. It is debatable

41

whether this event proves that Kaunas had already grown to be a town by this time. More reliable evidence is the fact that in 1408, on the eve of the Battle of Grünwald (Žalgiris in Lithuanian), Grand Duke Vytautas granted Kaunas a city charter.

After the combined Lithuanian-Polish forces defeated the Teutonic Order at Grünwald, Kaunas won the opportunity to use its strategic location for trade and business, not military purposes. Königsberg, Danzig and the other trading cities of the Hanseatic League were in the range of Kaunas' economic interests. Although Kaunas never joined the Hanseatic League, no other Lithuanian town could rival it in terms of its trading ties and volume.

Records from the 15th and 16th centuries indicate that by then, it was already well established as a commercial centre. However, its development was adversely affected by wars in the 17th century. The end of the 18th century, during the last decades of the independent statehood of the Grand Duchy of Lithuania, saw some decay in the city's standing.

The subsequent century of Russian rule left its traces in the life of the town. Many features,

still visible, remain in its architecture and place names. In the first three decades of the 19th century, when Vilnius was enjoying a measure of cultural autonomy and becoming a flourishing intellectual centre with one of the leading universities in the whole empire, Kaunas was very slowly rising from decay.

Only in the 20th century did Kaunas become a centre for political activity and democratic values. The Jewish community contributed to this metamorphosis. The names of Mapu, Zamenhof and Minkovskis, commemorated by the narrow lanes of Kaunas or Aleksotas (an old suburb of the city), are associated with the city's opening to a broader cultural heritage.

Kaunas as the Provisional Capital

Kaunas was influenced especially by events after the First World War. The establishment of the country's independent statehood, and the armed conflict with Poland, which led to the loss of Vilnius, made it the interim capital. This new status dramatically altered its identity in slightly more than a decade. Independ-

THE TOWN HALL IN THE OLD TOWN

ence transformed Kaunas from a provincial town into a capital with elegant architecture and an active intellectual life. At the end of the third decade, modern Bauhaus architecture appeared, a comfortable and modern urban structure was created, and cultural and scientific centres were founded and developed. The leading institutions included Vytautas Magnus University, the State Theatre,

KAUNAS SEMINARY

the Museum of War, and the M.K. Čiurlionis Art Museum. The industrial suburbs also grew rapidly.

The Unbroken Spirit of Kaunas

Kaunas is known for its stout resistance to Russification, which gave it its special character in Soviet times. The resistance movement was also stronger in Kaunas than anywhere else. The anti-Soviet demonstrations of 1956 and 1972 fortified the city's reputa-

tion, no less than the victories of the Žalgiris basketball team against the Soviet army team a decade later. For Lithuanians, as well as for some foreigners, Kaunas will always remain the city in which Romas Kalanta set himself on fire in 1972 to protest against Soviet oppression. Almost 25 years later this fact was recalled by Vaclav Havel, the Czech president and European statesman, who, during his visit to Kaunas, called on diplomats and officials to honour the place where Kalanta sacrificed his life. During the hippie movements, *Laisvės alėja* (Freedom Avenue), the central street, was a mecca for free-thinkers and individualists. Continuity was also ensured by the Catholic Church and the Kaunas seminary.

Kaunas is a city which jealously guards its traditions, yet looks towards the future. The forward-looking orientation of the city is strengthened by its tradition as a university city. Kaunas has nine university-level schools, including Vytautas Magnus University, the Medical University and Kaunas Technological University, which is the largest technical educational institution in the Baltic states. Over 24,000 students from around the country study in Kaunas. Their presence is especially felt on *Laisvės alėja,* or when the Kaunas Žalgiris team plays in Euroleague basketball championships. Young and old alike took part in an outpouring of joy when Žalgiris won the Euroleague championship in 1999.

Cultural Life

The cultural life of the city is enriched by seven professional theatres and the Philharmonic Hall. The Kaunas Jazz festival has been held every spring for nine years and has attracted international celebrities; Pažaislis Festival offers classical music concerts all summer at the Baroque Pažaislis monastery, which Lord Yehudi Menuhin was so fond of. Pažaislis also borders the Kaunas regional park, which, with its enormous man-made reservoir, is a place favoured by local residents for recreation.

Kaunas boasts 14 museums. Especially valuable pieces of fine and applied art are exhibited at the M. Žilinskas Art Gallery and the M.K. Čiurlionis Art Museum. The latter offers a chance to see the work of Čiurlionis, Lithuania's most distinguished artist. The Museum of Devils also enjoys great popularity: it holds a large collection of pieces of art and crafts representing the devil. After the re-establishment of independence, the Vytautas Magnus War Museum was modernised. A nearby garden, which was destroyed by the Soviets, has been restored. Today it hosts the Monument to Freedom, depicted as a neo-Classical goddess standing atop a towering pedestal. This is a popular place for commemorative meetings.

The Old Town

Town Hall Square is located at the heart of the Old Town, and is frequently the setting for festivals and concerts. It is dominated by the Baroque Town Hall (which the locals affectionately call the White Swan because of its graceful form and colour), dating from 1542. Nearby are the oldest churches: the Gothic Cathedral, the Holy Trinity Church, the Bernardine and Jesuit monasteries, the Vytautas Church (whose construction was begun at the beginning of the 15th century). Perkūnas House, a good example of Gothic, built at the end of the 15th century, was owned in turn by tradesmen and the Jesuits; it is currently used as the location for gymnasium art classes. The ruins of the 13th-century castle provide a striking backdrop for outdoor drama performances.

Kaunas has a multitude of parks. At the heart of the city is a 100-year-old oak grove with a zoo, established in 1938. At the other end of the city is the Botanical Garden, occupying 40 hectares, which was established in 1932.

The Economy

Kaunas is Lithuania's second largest city, inhabited by 414,200 people. Even during the late Soviet period the city had a reputation as a centre of private intitative and as home to numerous small sewing, fur, flower and trading enterprises. Kaunas' private traders travelled far and wide throughout the great expanse of the Soviet Union in search of customers and profits. Perhaps this is why Kaunas was known to have the highest rate of private automobile ownership of all cities in the Soviet Union.

Kaunas' position as the capital of small and medium-sized enterprises in Lithuania has not been lost. The city currently has about 20,000 commercial enterprises and some of the most dynamic new private companies.

Nevertheless, the importance of Lithuania's second city comes from its light industry, food processing and transport traditions. It has considerable economic potential by virtue of its convenient location, excellent transport links and diverse manufacturing base. The Via Baltica motorway, which links Helsinki with Central and Eastern Europe, passes through Kaunas. The four-lane motorway linking Klaipėda with Minsk and Moscow via Vilnius also skirts Kaunas. Lithuania's best air freight terminal is in Karmėlava, near Kaunas, and can receive every type of plane.

At the junction of all these transport corridors, a free economic zone will soon begin operations under the management of

KAUNAS' ŽALGIRIS WINS THE 1999 EUROLEAGUE BASKETBALL CHAMPIONSHIP

the Belgian company AOI; its shareholders include Antwerp port and the Belgian railways. The 1,050-hectare site is to include transport terminals as well as industrial enterprises, which will employ skilled Kaunas-based professionals in the electronics, metal processing, food and chemical sectors.

These branches of industry have already attracted significant investment, even before the inauguration of the free economic zone. Among the foreign investors active in Kaunas, are the following: Kraft Jacobs Suchard (confectionery), Pilsner Urquell (brewing), Tele Denmark International Cellular S.A., as well as a number of Western textile manufacturers.

Light industry and textiles are the traditional mainstay of Kaunas' economy. In fact, a considerable number of Lithuania's ready-to-wear clothing, fabrics, synthetic fibre and shoe enterprises are concentrated in Kaunas.

The city's expanding economic links abroad have also generated more interest among foreign businesses and, indirectly, tourists. Having fallen behind Vilnius somewhat in this respect, Kaunas is experiencing a modest rise in hotel construction and renovation. Three new hotels were completed in 1999. Many new upscale restaurants and shops have also recently opened, thereby making Lithuania's second city a more attractive location for foreign business.

THE KAUNAS WAR MUSEUM, A NOTABLE EXAMPLE OF PRE-WAR LITHUANIAN ARCHITECTURE

LAISVĖS ALĖJA, THE CENTRE OF KAUNAS

KLAIPĖDA PORT

KLAIPĖDA

Pop. 202,500

Distance from Vilnius – 318km

Klaipėda is Lithuania's gateway to the sea, and the most northerly ice-free port on the eastern coast of the Baltic Sea.

In the 13th century, a Baltic settlement had already been established in the area occupied by present-day Klaipėda, but it was destroyed by the Livonian Order, and a castle was erected in its place. The Germans mistook the Curonian Lagoon for the mouth of the River Nemunas, which they called Memel, and consequently named the new city Memel, too.

51

For a long time, the Klaipėda region was a province of Prussia, and even briefly became Prussia's capital in 1807. It was in Klaipėda that the decree on the abolition of serfdom in Prussia was promulgated.

After the First World War, control over Klaipėda and its district was transferred from Germany, in accordance with the Treaty of Versailles, and entrusted to France for temporary administration. During the insurrection of January 1923, Lithuanians occupied the Klaipėda district. A year later Klaipėda was placed under Lithuanian administration. Thus, about 430 years after the first trading vessels were built, the formerly sleepy port of Klaipėda experienced a burst of commercial activity. During the inter-war period, 80% of Lithuanian foreign trade went through Klaipėda port.

After the Second World War, Klaipėda became a centre for industry and fisheries. The port's average annual turnover of cargo increased to 20 million tonnes. In 1982, an international Klaipėda-

THEATRE SQUARE IN THE OLD TOWN

Mukran ferry was constructed, largely for military purposes. Today the ferry is used solely for the transport of commercial transit cargo.

The Port

Klaipėda follows a two to three-kilometre-wide strip along the Curonian Lagoon for about 15 kilometres. Klaipėda is Lithuania's third largest city, with 202,500 inhabitants. It is the largest industrial, cultural and educational centre in western Lithuania. The city enjoys good communications by sea (regular shipping lines connect it with Germany, Sweden, Denmark, the Netherlands, Great Britain, Belgium, Poland, Russia, Spain, Ecuador, Morocco, South Korea, the USA and Canada); by road (a 300-km motorway to Vilnius links it to the international Via Baltica motorway); and by air (the airport in Palanga is 25km away).

The main branches of the city's economy are sea transport, shipbuilding and ship repair, commercial fishing and fish processing, light industry and foodstuffs.

The city's largest enterprise is its port, visited by about 8,000 ships annually. The port can receive ships of up to 195 metres length and 10.5 metres draught. Klaipėda port's main cargoes include oil products, metals, fertilisers, timber and cement. These commodities amount to one fifth of the total turnover of the ports in this region.

The port is currently undergoing major expansion and renovation. The container terminal is being enlarged, the oil terminal improved, and the construction of special quays for dry cargo, a pas-

senger ferry terminal, and other terminals are planned. Deepening and widening of the waterways is envisaged. After this overhaul is complete, the port's annual capacity will increase to 30 million tonnes of cargo.

METAL CARGOES COMPRISE AN IMPORTANT PART OF KLAIPĖDA HARBOUR'S TOTAL VOLUME

Business in Klaipėda

In 1998, over 9,000 enterprises were registered in Klaipėda. The largest business volumes are recorded by LISCO (Lithuanian Shipping Company), KLASCO (Klaipėda Stevedoring Company), *Klaipėdos maistas* (meat products), *Klaipėdos mediena* (timber processing), *Klaipėdos nafta* (oil products terminal). The city boasts the oldest brewery in Lithuania, *Švyturys,* which was established in 1784. This enterprise is undergoing a massive modernisation programme financed by its new owner, the Danish Carlsberg. Baltijos Shipyard, also recently purchased by a Danish shipbuilder, is receiving considerable investment.

The city has attracted considerable investment by Philip Morris, Siemens, Master Foods/Mars and Lancaster Steel. More new investors will be attracted by the free economic zone, which is be-

54

ing established near the city. It will occupy an area of 205 hectares at a convenient transport junction.

For many centuries, Klaipėda lacked the chance to fully develop Lithuanian culture and education. Today the city has 54 educational institutions. Klaipėda University was established in 1991, and offers a wide range of courses. Klaipėda is also home to the Nautical Institute, the Visual Art Department of the Art Academy, and a conservatoire.

At the very end of the Curonian Peninsula is Kopgalis Fort, which houses the Maritime Museum, Aquarium and Dolphinarium, established in 1979. It is one of the richest and largest museums of its type in Europe. Also, the unique Museum of Clocks was established in Klaipėda 20 years ago, and exhibits items dating back to the 16th century. There are six theatres in Klaipėda.

Klaipėda offers easy access to the striking beauty and tranquillity of the Curonian Peninsula. Only 25 kilometres north of Klaipėda is the popular Palanga seaside resort, with its dunes and clean, white beaches.

HANDICRAFTS IN THE OLD TOWN

Šiauliai

ŠIAULIAI

Pop. 146,800

Distance from Vilnius – 230km

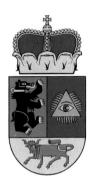

Despite its contemporary appearance, Šiauliai is one of Lithuania's oldest cities, first mentioned in historical documents in 1524. An important milestone in the history of Šiauliai is the Battle of Saulė in 1236, in which Lithuanian forces decisively defeated an invasion by the Livonian Order from Latvian territory. The city's fate has been much influenced by its geographic location: on the one hand, its location makes it a natural transport hub, on the other hand, it has found itself on the crossroads of military campaigns throughout history.

The 19th century was of exceptional importance for Šiauliai. The Riga-Tilsit road and Liepaja-Warsaw railway were constructed and passed through Šiauliai; and major industries were established. From the very beginning, leather processing enterprises assumed particular importance. In 1877, C. Frenkelis founded his leather works business (which today is known as the *Elnias* company), and in 1898 the Nurokai brothers established their leather enterprise (the present-day *Šiaulių Stumbras* company).

Today the economy of Šiauliai is dominated by trade as well as food and leather processing. As in the 19th century, the transport services sector constitutes a key element of the local economy. At the beginning of 1999, the city had 6,800 enterprises. In 1998, its industrial enterprises recorded sales totalling almost 0.5 billion litas (USD 125 million).

The *Rūta* confectionery firm was the first major enterprise in the city which, after more than a century, was returned to its legitimate owners. The joint Lithuanian-German *Baltik vairas* bicycle manufacturer has also adapted to the market economy: it remains a major producer in the city, and sold almost 160,000 bicycles in 1998, most of them in Western countries. Television assembly at the sprawling *Šiaulių tauras* enterprise, which formerly employed thousands of local people, fell on hard times in the first few years of independence, but has staged a significant recovery with the help of Danish investors.

There are 127 joint ventures with foreign capital participation, and 12 foreign capital enterprises in the city.

Šiauliai used to have one of the largest military airfields in the western part of the USSR. After the Soviet air force left in August 1993, its conversion into a civilian airport was started. The chief contractor for the conversion was the Dutch electronics giant Philips. The new airport was officially opened on 27 August 1997, and awarded the ICAO 1 category. It specialises in chartered flights and the development of aviation services. The airport's

THE A. GRICEVIČIUS COMPANY IN ŠIAULIAI IS THE OLDEST PRODUCER OF CONFECTIONERY IN LITHUANIA

significance has grown with the development of the nearby free economic zone. Šiauliai Airport is to become a transit point for air freight transported from Western Europe to Russia, Central Asia and the Far East. Freight terminals occupy an area of 3,000 square metres. Plans for the future include an air transport junction between East and West, based on the airport and the free economic zone. The Šiauliai Free Economic Zone occupies 457 hectares around the airport, and has excellent connections with major national roads and railways.

Šiauliai is the fourth largest city, both in area (813 sq km) and inhabitants (146,800), and is informally referred to as the capital of northern Lithuania.

The inhabitants of Šiauliai contemplated the idea of establishing a university 70 years ago, when Lithuania was forced to surrender the Vilnius and Klaipėda districts. These plans were finally realised in 1997. The new university at Šiauliai has about 5,600 BA, MA and doctoral students, most of them future teachers at schools of higher education.

The city also has a conservatoire, schools of medicine, technology, business and crafts. The Aušra Museum, which is a complex of smaller museums showing a wide variety of ethnographic, artistic and technical exhibits, is very popular in the north of Lithuania.

Algirdas Julius Greimas, a former professor at the Sorbonne, is one distinguished person whose roots were in Šiauliai. One would add Meyer Shapiro, a leading art historian; Aleksandra Fledžinskaitė-Kašubienė, an artist; the chamber orchestra conductor Saulius Sondeckis; the tenor Virgilijus Noreika; and the leading Lithuanian Catholic philosopher Stasys Šalkauskis.

Whenever visitors to Šiauliai ask about the city's history, locals think of Stanislava Jakševičiūtė-Venclauskienė, an actress and stage designer who worked on the first Lithuanian play in the city. She gave refuge to and brought up over a hundred homeless children. To commemorate her good deeds, the Monument to Motherhood was erected in 1993.

Šiauliai is the centre of the youngest diocese in the country (established in 1997). In spring, the city hosts popular festivals of church music.

In the mid 1970s, Vilnius Street was redesigned into a pedestrian zone. This was a pioneering move in the USSR, and attracted considerable interest and attention beyond Lithuania's borders.

POPE JOHN PAUL II CELEBRATED
MASS AT THE HILL OF CROSSES.
SEPTEMBER, 1993.

The Hill of Crosses

Not far from Šiauliai is Jurgaičiai Hill, also known as the Hill of Crosses, one of the most revered sites for the country's faithful. On 7 September 1993 Pope John Paul II acknowledged its importance as a symbol of resistance to religious persecution by viSsiting it.

The Hill of Crosses originated in 1847, when an inhabitant of the village of Jurgaičiai fell seriously ill and resolved to erect a cross on the nearby hill if he recovered. He did, his story became widely known, and three years later there were already 20 crosses standing on the hill. After the rebellion of 1863, when the Tsarist administration prohibited the display of crosses near houses and on roads, the hill became unrecognisable: Lithuanians en masse started putting up crosses to commemorate those killed in the uprising, and those exiled to Siberia. During the Soviet era, the hill was first razed by tractors and fire in 1961. Over 5,000 crosses were destroyed. Today a veritable sea of crosses – hundreds of thousands of them – serves as a monument to Lithuanians' attachment to their religion.

SAULĖS LAIKRODŽIO AIKŠTĖ (SUNDIAL SQUARE) WITH ŠAULYS, THE SYMBOL OF THE CITY

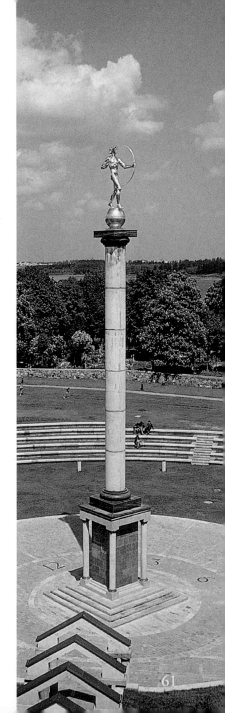

PANEVĖŽYS

PANEVĖŽYS
Pop. 133,700
Distance from Vilnius – 145km

Panevėžys is the fifth largest city, an administrative centre, informally referred to as the capital of the Aukštaitija region. The city occupies an area of 50 square kilometres close to the River Nevėžis. Compared with other Lithuanian cities, Panevėžys is the most densely inhabited. Its population also has the highest percentage of ethnic Lithuanians (92%) of all major Lithuanian cities.

Altogether, 25% of the working population is employed at industrial enterprises, which produce 80% of the city's domestic product.

Although Panevėžys is surrounded by good agricultural land, it remains chiefly an industrial city, with over 6,500 registered enterprises.

Panevėžys is well known for its TV and electronic equipment, glass and pottery, textiles and clothing. Production is exported to over 50 different countries.

The city has 77 joint Lithuanian-foreign capital ventures, with companies from Scandinavia, Germany, the USA and Ireland. The largest foreign investment so far has been in *Kalnapilis*, which produces beer and non-alcoholic beverages. A Swedish-Finnish consortium has invested 84 million litas in the modernisation of *Kalnapilis*. *Ekranas*, which produces TV screens and other electrical components (with Swiss investments of 74 million litas) is another major joint venture with foreign capital.

63

A number of Panevėžys construction companies have earned a solid reputation in Lithuania and are involved in many of the major construction projects currently in progress throughout the country. The linen producer *Linas* exports its fabrics to almost every continent: it can produce up to eight million square metres of cloth a year.

About 15% of the city's population is employed in small and medium-sized enterprises. The city has a Chamber of Trade, Industry and Crafts, and a Business Consulting Centre.

Panevėžys is located astride the main Vilnius to Riga road, which on the Lithuanian side is largely a modern, four-lane highway. A military airfield close to the city is due to be used for commercial purposes.

Panevėžys was founded in 1503. It is twinned with a number of cities in Western Europe: Oss in the Netherlands, Lünen in Germany, and Kalmar in Sweden. International relations broadened after the Balto-Scandian (Baltic-Scandinavian) Academy

*THE **KALNAPILIS** BREWERY OF PANEVĖŽYS WAS THE FIRST LITHUANIAN BREWERY MODERNISED WITH THE HELP OF FOREIGN CAPITAL*

was established in 1991, which is known for its international cultural conferences, literary research and library.

For many years, Panevėžys was famous for the Juozas Miltinis Drama Theatre. Miltinis, a theatre director and disciple of Charles Dullin, studied in France from 1932 to 1937. He was one of the founders of modern Lithuanian theatre and a great innovator. In the Soviet period his productions regularly brought theatregoers to Panevėžys from major cities and faraway corners of the Soviet Union.

Panevėžys is a city of theatres. Besides the Miltinis Drama Theatre, it has the Menas family drama theatre, a unique mobile puppet theatre, the Musical Theatre of Masks and Puppets, the Musical Theatre, and the Theatre of Poetry.

The city attracts students to the A. Domaševičius Medical School, a higher technical school, the Panevėžys Conservatoire, the Music School, 20 high schools, and two gymnasiums. Panevėžys hopes to establish a university of its own.

The cultural heritage of the Aukštaitija region and Lithuania in general is collected and preserved for future generations by the Museum of Ethnography.

Modern art can be viewed at the Algimantas Gallery of photographic art, Gallery XX and Gallery Second Floor. Each spring the city hosts professional art festivals. In autumn, Panevėžys becomes the venue for an annual international vocal jazz festival. The name of Panevėžys has become well known to potters from Japan, the USA and European countries thanks to an annual international pottery symposium which has been organised over the past ten years by the Art Gallery and the glass plant.

September 7, the "Day of the City" is a special one for the inhabitants of Panevėžys. On this occasion, distinguished residents receive awards, exhibitions of industrial products are held, galleries and other institutions open their doors and meetings, festivities and sporting events take place throughout the city.

In September 1999, the 100th anniversary of the narrow-gauge railway will be commemorated. This unique railway, beginning in Panevėžys and ending at Anykščiai, winds its way through the picturesque uplands of northeastern Lithuania.

PALANGA HAS OPEN SPACES...

PALANGA
Pop. 19,600
Distance from Vilnius – 338km

Palanga is Lithuania's premier seaside resort, with long stretches of sandy beach, dunes and a large botanical garden. It can (and does) accommodate over 100,000 holidaymakers at a time in the season (June-August). In spring and summer, Palanga enjoys more sunny days than most

AND SOME VERY POPULAR BEACHES

other places in Lithuania. It has over 200 guest facilities, including many modest-sized hotels and inns built in the last five years, 11 sanatoria, recuperation centres, and the well-known Health School.

Palanga was first mentioned in historical writings in 1161. Originally it was a fishing village. From the 15th to the 17th century, Palanga developed into Lithuania's main port, and even competed for sea cargo with Klaipėda and Riga. The first Lithuanian play, Keturakis' *America in the Bathhouse*, was staged in Palanga in 1899.

Palanga became famous as a health resort in the 19th century, after Count Tiškevičius purchased an extensive estate on the fringes of the town in 1824. Soon

67

after, the first guest villas sprang up, a park at Birutė Hill was laid out, and a stately mansion was erected. Today the building houses the Museum of Amber, which holds the largest collection of rare pieces of amber in the world.

At the beginning of this century, Palanga became a popular health resort, favoured by the aristocracy of Lithuania, Poland and Russia.

Each year the opening of the summer season is celebrated at the beginning of June. The town has numerous other festivals and concerts. In July, the Aviation Festival is held at Palanga Airport. Since 1971, open-air concerts of chamber music, called Night Serenades, have been held on the terrace of the Tiškevičius Palace. A new artistic programme, Classical Season in Palanga Park, started in the summer of 1998.

THE TIŠKEVIČIUS PALACE HAS AN EXTENSIVE AMBER COLLECTION AND A BEAUTIFUL PARK

DRUSKININKAI
Pop. 21,700
Distance from Vilnius – 132km

The oldest health resort, located in the very south of the country, is known for its natural charm. The town of Druskininkai grew up around the mineral springs, which have drawn health seekers there for several centuries. In 1794, Stanislovas Augustas, the king of Poland and Lithuania, issued a decree officially designating Druskininkai a health resort. The first sanatoria appeared in the 19th century, and their numbers subsequently increased.

Druskininkai is a year-round health resort and a centre for tourism. The pride of the town is its seven mineral springs. Among other things, their waters cure disorders of the digestive tract, normalise the functions of the stomach and improve the workings of the liver. Peat mud has a curative effect on gynaecological condi-

ROADSIDE FOLK SCULPTURES NEAR DRUSKININKAI

tions, joints, vertebrae, the metabolism, and nervous system disorders. Nine sanatoria and a 200-bed health resort function all year round. Besides these cures, they also offer climate therapy and therapeutic gymnastics.

THE PICTURESQUE ENVIRONS OF DRUSKININKAI

Pine trees, sand, the River Nemunas, the Ratnyčia and several lakes create a very special microclimate. The picturesque surroundings of Druskininkai and the neighbouring Dzūkija National Park offer tourists many possibilities for active recreation, including hiking, cycling and canoeing.

Druskininkai is the city of Mikalojus Konstantinas Čiur-

lionis, an artist and composer, and has a museum devoted to him. *Girios aidas* is a museum founded by the Lithuanian Union of Foresters. The health resort is known for its traditional dance marathons, autumn poetry festival, days of chamber music for young people, and artists' symposia. The "Day of Druskininkai" is celebrated on the last weekend of May. There are plans to establish an unusual and controversial exhibition of sculptures and monuments left over from the Soviet era close to Druskininkai.

TRADITIONAL WINDMILLS COME IN MANY SHAPES

71

Neringa

Pop. 2,700
Distance from Vilnius – 338km

The main settlements on the Lithuanian section of the Curonian Peninsula, Nida, Preila, Pervalka, Juodkrantė and Alksnynė, are

NIDA SEEN FROM THE TOP OF PARNIDIS DUNE

grouped together in a single administrative unit, the town of Neringa. The peninsula is a unique phenomenon with its sand dunes, beach coastline and fragrant pine forests. About 12% of the peninsula consists of dunes. The German writer Thomas Mann, who visited Nida briefly in August 1929, wrote in his *Life Sketches*: "We were very much fascinated by the uniqueness of the nature, its beauty, the world of fantastic, moving dunes, be-

yond any description". Later he built a summer house in Nida, and spent the summers of 1930 to 1932 there writing *Joseph and his Brothers.*

Almost 200 rare and protected plants can be found on the peninsula, which has been set aside as a nature preserve. The traditional fishermen's houses are covered with roofs of thatch and tiles. Horse head-shaped weather-cocks remind the visitor that fishing is the traditional occupation of the locals, which has penetrated their lives and spiritual culture. In Smiltynė and Nida, *kurėnai,* old wooden sailing vessels of the Curonian fishermen, can be seen anchored offshore in the lagoon. In the evening, the smell of smoked fish wafts over the fishermen's houses.

Before the Second World War, the settlement of Juodkrantė was a health resort fairly well known in Europe. It is one of the oldest settlements on the Curonian Peninsula.

Neringa, an oasis of peace, combines the beauty of nature with the advantages of civilisation. It offers clean beaches, and

THE SAND DUNES NEAR NIDA ARE SPECTACULAR

diverse landscapes. A visitor can climb Parnidis Dune with its sun-dial and calendar, or walk among the wooden folk sculptures on *Raganų kalnas* (Witches' Hill). Other points of interest in Nida are the Thomas Mann Museum and the Amber Gallery. A bicycle route has recently been built through much of Nida.

A 2,400-metre quay has been built in Juodkrantė. A small harbour is also now available to receive motorboats and yachts. In 1997, the first sculptures produced by artists attending the annual international symposium of sculptors were installed on the quay at Juodkrantė. Here, guests can enjoy the walk along the promenade following the contours of the bay.

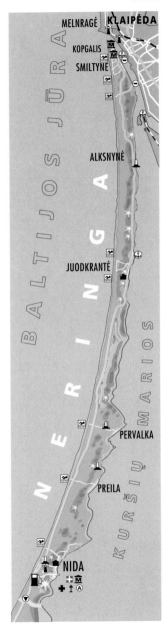

⊕ PORT
🛱 LIGHTHOUSE
⊖ FERRY
🏖 BEACH
⚱ MONUMENT, MEMORIAL
✳ IMPORTANT HILL
🚻 HOSPITAL
🏛 INTERESTING BUILDING
Ⓐ BUS TERMINAL
🏛 MUSEUM, EXHIBITION HALL
† CEMETERY
▼ CUSTOMS
✚ CHURCH, CHAPEL
🛢 FILLING STATION

De Oost Zee,

SINVS MAGNVS LIVONIÆ

MAGNI LITHVÆ CÆTERARVMQVE ILLI ADIACENTIVM EXACTA DEscriptio Ex Archetypo quodam Christophori Radziuil, per Ducem illius Impensas et ex Mss Consilio nuntiatum Adiuta operâ Gerardi Mercatoris

LI:
VO:
NIÆ
PARS.

CVR:
LAN:
DIÆ
DVCATVS.

SAMOGITIA

SEMIG

BALTICVM
MARE

PRVSSIA

Königsberg

Vilna

CVIAVIÆ
PROVINCIÆ MAIORIS POLONIÆ
PARS

Pod:
la
chi
a

Polesia

Volynia

Russia

MINORIS
Lublin

POLONIÆ

tru

Si
RI

SIGNORVM vel
CARACTERVM DECLARATIO
Vrbs
Ciuitas
Ciuitas iudicialis ad districtendis urbs zonae solidum disperguntur
Dominicum Durum
Sedes Episcopi Romani
Sedes Episcopi Græcorum quae vulgo Wladicae appellatur
Oppidum
Pagus cum domo Nobilis

Amstelodami
Sumptibus Guilielmi Ianssonius sub signo
Solaris Anno 1613

CRACOVIA

Sculptum
apud Herschenn
Geranium.

Milliaria magna
Milliaria mediocria
Milliaria communia siue Gallica

Pokutiæ pars

HISTORY

Lithuania lies between Western and Eastern Europe on a direct route from Germany to Russia. It was through Lithuania that the Germans forced their way eastwards during the Middle Ages and in this century. The Russians also used this route to extend their power westwards. Although it is at the geographic centre of Europe, Lithuania is sometimes considered to be a part of Eastern Europe. This view was justified not by the country's geographic, but rather by its geopolitical situation: in the 19th and 20th centuries it was occupied and annexed by its Eastern neighbour. In terms of civilisation, however, Lithuania belongs to Central Europe. Here, in contrast to Eastern Europe, from the Middle Ages onward, the peasantry lived and worked on individual farms and not in communal villages; a civil society came into existence, as opposed to Oriental-style despotic rule; Catholicism

77

and a Western cultural outlook prevailed instead of the Orthodox tradition. Modern Lithuania is oriented towards Central, Northern and Western Europe and enjoys good relations with all its neighbours.

MILESTONES IN LITHUANIA'S HISTORY

Lithuania was first mentioned in historical records in 1009. A state, the Grand Duchy of Lithuania, was established in the middle of the 13th century. This state, which developed ever-closer relations with Poland, existed until the end of the 18th century, when it was annexed by Russia. In 1918 Lithuania reemerged as the independent Republic of Lithuania. The Soviet Union occupied Lithuania in 1940, inflicting enormous losses on the population in the process of consolidating its hold. The Second World War witnessed the Holocaust of Lithuanian Jews, mass Soviet deportations to Siberia and mass emigration to the West. Lithuania was annexed and ruled by the Soviet Union for half a century until 1990. Soviet perestroika gave vent to pent up national longings for freedom, which culminated in a peaceful and successful drive for the restoration of independence, for a second time this century.

THE ANCIENT BALTS AND THEIR LEGACY

The term Balts, as used in academic research, usually applies to the group of Indo-European tribes and peoples who lived, or still live, on the eastern coast of the Baltic Sea. Balts speak related languages that belong to a distinct branch of the Indo-European group of languages. Today, only the Lithuanian and Latvian languages survive. The Balts have been settled near the Baltic Sea for at least 4,000 years. They are therefore considered to be among the oldest and most settled European peoples.

The Baltic tribes started forming at the end of the third millennium BC, when invading Indo-Europeans became assimilated with the previously settled people. In the first millennium AD the area inhabited by the Baltic tribes reached as far as the Dniepr and Oka rivers. Later, in the second half of the first millennium, the expansion of Slavic tribes started, which ended with the assimilation of the eastern Balts.

At the beginning of the second millennium, the Prussian, Jotvingian, Lithuanian and Latvian nations started to emerge. However, only the Lithuanians and Latvians survived as nations; the Prussians and Jotvingians were conquered and assimilated by the Teutonic Order, which later established the Prussian state.

It is perhaps due to the settled Baltic lifestyle that Baltic mythology has preserved many features of ancient Indo-European mythology. A. Meillet (1866–1936), a French linguist, remarked: "If one wants to hear how our grandparents spoke, one should come and listen to a Lithuanian peas-

KEY DATES	
1009	*Bruno of Querfurt discovers Lithuania.*
1253 (6 July)	*Mindaugas is crowned king.*
1385	*Jogaila, Grand Duke of Lithuania, becomes King of Poland. Lithuanian-Polish rapprochement begins.*
1387	*The baptism of Lithuania.*
1392–1430	*The reign of Vytautas the Great.*
1410	*The Battle of Žalgiris (Grünwald). The joint Lithuanian-Polish forces defeat the Teutonic Order .*
1569	*The Lublin Union. A Polish-Lithuanian state is established.*
1795	*Russia, Austria and Prussia divide among themselves the Polish-Lithuanian state.*
1918 (16 February)	*The Council of Lithuania proclaims the restoration of an independent Lithuanian state.*
1940 (15 June)	*The Soviet Union occupies and annexes the Republic of Lithuania.*
1941–1944	*Lithuania is occupied by Germany.*
1944–1953	*The Soviet Union carries out organised persecution, mass deportations and forced collectivisation. Lithuania's armed resistance movement.*
1990 (11 March)	*The Supreme Council of the Republic of Lithuania declares the restoration of Lithuania's independence.*

ant." As Lithuania converted to Christianity relatively late, the national culture and traditions are full of features inherited from pagan times. They have even entered Christian holiday traditions. The remains of these ancient elements are responsible for the uniqueness of Lithuanian folklore and folk art.

THE "DISCOVERY" OF LITHUANIA IN 1009

The first millennium AD was the era of Baltic fragmentation. As early as the second century AD, Ptolemy was aware of the Prussian, Galindian, Jotvingian and Suduvian tribes. In the early Middle Ages scribes started mentioning the Prussians, Curonians and Semigallians.

In 1009 a Western missionary, Bruno of Querfurt, travelled from Prussia to Lithuania to baptise a Lithuanian chief named Netimeras. Unfortunately, the latter was killed by his own brother shortly thereafter. Nevertheless, one may infer that Netimeras' political status meant that Lithuania had reached at least the stage of a chiefdom. This fact suggests that there was no essential difference at the time between Lithuania and the other Central and Northern European countries (which also attracted Christian missionaries). However, the mission of Bruno in 1009 and the discovery of Lithuania remain only fragments of historical knowledge. Lithuania was hardly mentioned in historical records in the following 200 years.

THE FOUNDING OF THE STATE AND MINDAUGAS' CORONATION

At the end of the 12th century Lithuania reemerged in historical documents. This was caused by heightened military activity by the Lithuanians aimed at Russia, Poland, the neighbouring Balts and the Estonians. At the same time, the Teutonic orders started settling on the Baltic shores. In 1200 the Knights of the Sword settled at the mouth of the River Daugava and conquered the Lyvians, Latvians, Estonians and Curonians. In 1230 the Knights of the Cross settled on the River Vistula and then subjugated the Prussians. In 1236 the Pope called for a crusade against the pagan Lithuanians.

Thus the emergence in 1240 of the Lithuanian state under the rule of Mindaugas was a defensive response to the crusades in the Baltic lands and the appearance of the German military orders. At the time, however, Christendom tried to deny pagan tribes the right to an independent political existence. This principle applied to almost every pagan tribe and nation that lived between the Catholic and the Byzantine world, including the Slavs, Prussians, Jotvingians, Curonians, Latvians, Estonians and Finns.

Mindaugas, therefore, accepted baptism in 1251 and was crowned king on 6 July 1253. He thus formally became a servant of the Pope. Nevertheless, the crown did not come cheaply: Mindaugas was forced to hand over Žemaitija (Samogitia), an important part of Lithuania, to the Order. The Samogitians never accepted this. They continued to resist the Order, and even defeated it in 1260 at the Battle of Durbė.

Political immaturity, instability and intrigues characterised the Lithuanian state at the time. Conspirators murdered Mindaugas in 1263. He was the first, and the last, Lithuanian king.

PAGAN LITHUANIA

At first glance, Mindaugas' Christian state appeared to be only temporary. Nevertheless, the state continued to exist, even though its subsequent rulers were not baptised. In this respect, it became unique in Europe, belonging neither to the Roman-based Western Europe nor the Byzantine Eastern Europe.

Individual farms – the foundation of Western European civilisation – emerged in Lithuania over the course of history, in contrast to developments in Eastern Europe. Moreover, after Mindaugas' death, Lithuanian rulers all negotiated the issue of baptism. This was caused by the conflicts with the Teutonic Order. At the end of the 13th century the Teutonic Order commenced military action against Lithuania, after conquering the neighbouring Prussians.

It was quite obvious that the cost of accepting baptism by the Teutonic Order was far too high. Therefore, alternative kinds of baptism were sought, namely from the Czechs, Hungary and Poland (baptism in the Orthodox tradition would not have solved the problem of armed attacks by the Order).

Gediminas, Grand Duke of Lithuania (1316–1341), sought to break out of international isolation by corresponding extensively with the rulers of Western countries and cities. This, along with baptism and his attempts to attract Western traders and artisans, did not produce immediate results. The Order's aggression forced Lithuania to allocate all of its resources to defence. Therefore, the country's political system in the 14th century is sometimes referred to as a military monarchy.

On the other hand, it was in the military field that the country exercised its greatest influence on its neighbours. The "Lithuanian shield" was known and used in diplomacy from Moscow to the Czech lands.

The crusades against Lithuania explain to some extent Lithuania's expansion into the Kievan Rus lands,which were weakened by the Mongols. This was a way of gathering resources for the struggle in the west. During the rule of Grand Duke Algirdas (1345–1377), Lithuania not only became a major power but also extended its territory from the Baltic to the Black Sea.

It became a dual state, with ethnic Lithuanian lands as well as far more extensive and populated Slavic lands. Here a distinct and independent (from Moscow) Slavic identity – Ruthenian – developed in the course of time. In these lands Lithuanians discovered what they had been lacking themselves: a culture with a religious system and a written language. These circumstances explain the important role of Orthodox culture in Lithuania's early history. Local Lithuanian dukes who became governors in the Slavic lands adopted the Orthodox religion. At the same time, the emerging Ruthenian written language gradually became the official language of administration in the Grand Duchy of Lithuania.

This situation was similar to that of the Franks in Gallic lands.

MOSCOW

BALTIC SEA

VILNIUS

Eastern border of modern Lithuania

KIEV

KRAKOW

LITHUANIA
and
POLAND
in the 1st part of XV c.

BLACK SEA

The Franks, a German tribe, established a state and government institutions in Gallic territories, but took on the local language and culture. Lithuanians brought to Ruthenian lands government structures, military architecture, farming practices and a certain degree of prosperity related to the latter.

THE BAPTISM OF EUROPE'S LAST PAGANS (1387)

In the second half of the 14th century the Teutonic Order's military attacks against Lithuania reached unprecedented proportions - up to four campaigns a year. The country's resources were stretched, and a solution was desperately needed. One was found: in 1385 Lithuania and Poland concluded the Krėva Agreement, according to which Jogaila, Grand Duke of Lithuania, became King of Poland. One of the provisions of the agreement was that Lithuania subject itself to baptism. This was carried out in 1387 after Jogaila returned from Poland. Jogaila thereupon unleashed a campaign of his own against expressions of the old faith: the worship of holy woods, grass snakes and sacred fire.

Political circumstances played a major role in Lithuania's acceptance of the Catholic faith. The usefulness of baptism was revealed immediately after the Pope prohibited the Teutonic Order from waging war against Lithuania. From that moment, the Order could not expect any more significant support from the West. This circumstance, as well as the alliance with Poland by virtue of the Krėva Agreement, laid the groundwork for the victory at the Battle of Grünwald (Žalgiris).

In 1410, a combined Polish-Lithuanian army went on the offensive, penetrating the lands of the Teutonic Order and confronting its forces. It was one of the greatest battles of the Middle Ages, in which the joint army won an impressive victory that ensured the permanent defeat of the Teutonic Order.

Thus, by accepting baptism and conquering the Order, Lithuania freed itself from a persistent threat to its existence. A new stage in its history unfolded, one which decisively pointed Lithuania towards Central Europe.

TURNING TO THE WEST

At the Battle of Grünwald, the Lithuanian and Polish forces were led by Vytautas the Great (1392–1430), the preeminent political figure in Lithuanian history. It was during his rule that the foundations were laid for the country's orientation towards Central Europe, which is referred to by historians as a civilisation leap. Lithuania was obliged to assimilate, over a very short period, the institutions and intellectual heritage that had ripened gradually in medieval Western Europe: crop rotation, the feudal system and monarchy, craft guilds, the religious system, schools and the role of the written language.

Lithuania managed to achieve this over a period of about 150 years. A key role in this learning process was played by Lithuanian students studying in Cracow and later German and Italian universities.

JAN MATEJKO (1838-1893). THE BATTLE OF GRÜNWALD.

These studies, and the acceptance of European values, started producing tangible results by the end of the 15th century. In 1499 the first book prepared in Lithuania was printed abroad; in 1500 a Gothic masterpiece, St Anne's Church, was erected in Vilnius; in 1522 the printing of books started in Lithuania; in 1529 an advanced legal code, the Lithuanian Statute, was completed; in 1547 the first book written in Lithuanian was published.

In the middle of the 16th century Lithuania reacted strongly to the challenges of the Reformation, which signifies that it was already actively participating as a state within European structures.

Generally during this period, Lithuania and Poland were governed by the same rulers, although formally they remained separate states. This phenomenon is known as a personal union. Both the Lithuanian and Polish thrones were held by the Jagiellonian (Jogaila) dynasty until 1572. In the late 15th and early 16th centuries, this dynasty also occupied the Czech and Hungarian thrones.

Thus, the eastern part of Central Europe in this time was called Jagiellonian Europe, and the Jagiellonian dynasty was a major rival of the Habsburgs. Even more importantly, during this era Lithuania and Jagiellonian Europe played an "antemurale christianitatis" role, although not always successfully. If Lithuania, with Poland's help, managed to defeat Moscow in the Battle of Orsha in 1514, Hungary was less successful and was itself overcome by the Turks at the Battle of Mohacs in 1526. After the Battle of Mohacs, Hungary disappeared from the map of Europe, and the Jagiellonian dynasty was deprived of the Czech lands.

Only Lithuania and Poland remained. But Lithuania's civilisation leap and its political rapprochement with Poland also facilitated the Polonisation of its society and culture, although this process can hardly be thought of

as a hostile cultural intrusion. The Grand Duchy's elites voluntarily adopted the Polish language and its culture.

A third factor was the influence of Ruthenian society on the Grand Duchy of Lithuania. As this part of society was integrating into the elites of the Grand Duchy, it became obvious that the Ruthenian language (related to Polish) was a far more effective means of communicating with the court of the grand duke than the Lithuanian language. The Lithuanian elites, through the use of Ruthenian, moved towards the use of Polish, while preserving Lithuanian national self-awareness. Only later would the Polish language oust Ruthenian completely, and the Lithuanian ruling elements would become conscious of the Polonia nostra concept. That was largely caused by the creation of the Polish-Lithuanian state.

THE 1569 LUBLIN UNION AND THE ESTABLISHMENT OF THE POLISH-LITHUANIAN STATE

In the late 15th and early 16th centuries, wars between Moscow and Lithuania developed into a struggle over Livonia. It became obvious that Lithuania was not strong enough to stand on its own. This prompted the Lithuanians to enter into an even closer union with Poland. In 1569, in the Polish city of Lublin, Lithuania and Poland established a union which created a new state, the Republic of the Two Nations.

By then Lithuania, through its crippling wars with Moscow, had lost a large part of its territory in what is now Ukraine, and some of its sovereignty as well. From that time onwards, Polish kings automatically became grand dukes of Lithuania. The Lublin Union created the Seimas, a Polish-Lithuanian parliament of nobles, in which Lithuania held one third of the seats.

This erosion of the country's sovereignty explains why Poland became much more visible than Lithuania in Europe in the 17th and 18th centuries. In foreign historiography the joint state was referred to simply as Poland. This view is mistaken, as Lithuania preserved its independent executive power, its military, legal and financial systems.

Moreover, the new parliamentary order of nobles, based on the *liberum veto* (which in effect gave each deputy veto power), limited Polish influence over Lithuania. Therefore, the Polish-Lithuanian relationship after the

Lublin Union is best described as a confederation.

The consequences of the Lublin Union became visible shortly afterwards. After the Polish-Lithuanian throne was taken by Steponas Batoras, an energetic Transylvanian duke (who ruled from 1576 to 1586), crucial victories were won against Mos-

ST JOHN CAPISTRANO BEFORE GRAND DUKE OF LITHUANIA AND KING OF POLAND KAZIMIERAS JOGAILAITIS - UNKNOWN ARTIST

cow, and this threat was deferred for half a century. In fact from 1609 to 1611, Lithuania and Poland even managed to occupy Moscow.

THE BAROQUE ERA

Lithuania's integration into Western European civilisation in the 16th century paved the way for its status as an integral part of Central Europe in the 17th and 18th centuries. Northern and Western Europe marched rapidly towards a modern society, free enterprise and the ideas of the Enlightenment, whereas the rest of Europe remained agricultural, feudal and Catholic.

Lithuania's history in the 17th and 18th centuries is described as the Baroque era. Its symbolic beginning is 1569. The defining event, however, was not the Lublin Union, but rather the appearance in Lithuania of the Jesuits, the leading ideological and spiritual power of the period. The Jesuits brought a revitalised Catholic tradition and, with the state's assistance, introduced higher standards to education.

A network of schools was created, crowned by Vilnius University (its official title being Academia et Universitas Vilnensis Societatis Jesu). Founded in 1579, it is sometimes referred to as the oldest university in Eastern Europe. A more precise description would be to call it the last university belonging to the medieval tradition of universities. For almost 200 years, it was the most easterly Western-style university (Moscow University was founded only in 1755).

Vilnius University, which had two faculties, Philosophy and Law, developed distinguished schools of poetics and rhetoric, history and philology, and philosophy and logic. Perhaps the clearest indication of its high calibre is a volume on logic written by Martynas Smigleckis (1618), which was used as a textbook in Western European universities as well.

If in the 15th and 16th centuries Lithuania adopted Gothic and Renaissance architecture late and incoherently, in the 17th and 18th centuries it became a country of Baroque architecture, which still delights visitors. In the 17th century Italian Baroque dominated; whereas in the 18th century an independent Vilnius School of Baroque emerged. The architect J. Glaubicas, the outstanding proponent of this school, deserves a place in the history of European Baroque. It was during this period that the Baroque profile of Vilnius' Old Town was formed: a town which belongs to the string of Baroque cities stretching from Salzburg to Vilnius.

Nevertheless, the rural nature of society and the underdevelopment of the cities produced a unique kind of estate system – a democracy of nobles, perhaps even a kind of anarchy. According to the *liberum veto* rule, all decisions in the parliament of nobles had to be taken unanimously. This contrasted with Western European absolutist regimes and, at the same time, prevented Poland-Lithuania from strengthening and centralising the state.

Such an anachronistic state of affairs also had the beneficial effect of promoting the co-existence of various religious communities: Catholics lived together with Calvinists, Lutherans, Unitarians and Orthodox believers. Later these were joined by Old Believers from Russia and also by Karaites, Tartars and Jews.

The latter group had an especially significant influence on that era and during Lithuania's subsequent history. In the 18th century, Vilnius became a leading world centre for Jewish culture, and was referred to as the Lithuanian Jerusalem.

Unfortunately, the country's growth and orientation towards European Baroque culture was regularly impeded by its neighbours. During the rule of the Swedish Vasa dynasty (1587–1668), Lithuania and Poland experienced what was called "The Flood", an invasion of Russian and Swedish troops lasting from 1654 to 1667. Under the Saxonian dynasty (1697–1763), the country became the battleground for the Northern War (1700–1721) pitting Russia against Sweden.

The consequence of this war was Russia's direct interference in the Lithuanian-Polish state's internal affairs, which finally resulted in the division and liquidation of the Polish-Lithuanian Republic.

THE 1791 CONSTITUTION AND ITS ABOLITION

The expansion of Russia led to the first partition of 1772, which also involved Austria and Prussia. Perhaps responding to these circumstances as well as to the spread of the Enlightenment, the state undertook reforms aimed at strengthening its powers. One obvious target was the anarchic democracy of nobles, which was incapable of adapting to political change.

These attempts culminated in the Constitution of 3 May 1791, which was passed by the Polish-Lithuanian Seimas. It abolished the *liberum veto* principle. For the first time, residents of the towns gained the right of political representation in parliament; the state started to regulate the relations between landowners and peasants; a hereditary monarchy was proclaimed.

In a European and global context these endeavours may seem unremarkable. But it is notable that the Polish-Lithuanian Constitution proclaimed that the hereditary monarchy expressed the will of the people. In this respect, the Constitution was based on the order introduced in England over a hundred years previously. Al-

VILNIUS ENVIRONS: ANTAKALNIS. 1848 LITHOGRAPH BY ALPHONSE BICHEBOIS. FROM A DRAWING BY KANUT RUSIECKI

though the Polish-Lithuanian Constitution was adopted later than the American Constitution of 1783, it preceded the French Constitution by a few months.

The French document in fact played an important role in the minds of the drafters of the Polish-Lithuanian Constitution. Writing to the French Constituent Assembly in the summer of 1791, Stanisław-August Poniatowski, the ruler of Poland-Lithuania, noted that, along with France, "yet another nation has appeared in Europe."

Although the world and even Lithuanians think of this Consti-

tution as the Constitution of Poland, Lithuania nevertheless secured an important amendment to this document in the autumn of 1791. Lithuania could claim half of all the offices in government institutions throughout the land. The Constitution was created to bury the old Polish-Lithuanian order and was largely based on the system created by the French Revolution. It therefore provoked strong opposition, mainly by the aristocracy and Catherine the Great of Russia.

Lithuanian reactionary forces sought help from Russia which, together with Prussia, obliged by carrying out the second partition of Poland-Lithuania in 1793, and forcing Stanisław-August to abolish the Constitution. This move was opposed by Polish and Lithuanian society, which rose up in arms. The uprising was led by Tadeusz Kościuszko, a hero of the American War of Independence. Nevertheless, the revolution was crushed by the Russian military commander Suvorov.

Thus Russia, Prussia and Austria carried out the third partition of Poland-Lithuania in 1795, after which it disappeared from the political map of Europe. Lithuania was annexed by Russia. Despite this setback, the Constitution of 3 May became a guiding light for Lithuanian society as it modernised the country in the 19th century. The fact that Lithuania became a modern society and managed to recover its statehood in 1918 owes much to the developments of 1791.

MODERNISATION UNDER RUSSIAN OPPRESSION

Following the partitions, Lithuania for the first time in its history fell under the rule of a truly alien foreign power. This situation continued for over a hundred years. Lithuania only recovered its statehood at the end of the First World War, which brought with it a wave of collapsing empires in Europe. The country's incorporation into Russia revealed very clearly that the new master, in spite of its pro-European claims voiced since the days of Peter the Great, was far less European than Lithuania itself.

Never before in Lithuanian history had family members living in feudal dependence been subject to separation by their masters as they now were under Tsarist domination. Russia also abolished the democratic principles and reforms which had taken root in 1791. On the other hand, there were other indications that both Lithuania and Russia were moving towards creating Euro-

pean societies. An important breakthrough was the abolition of serfdom in 1861.

In Lithuania, the limited abolition of serfdom failed to supply the newly liberated peasants with land and had unexpected consequences, including a widespread uprising. This was suppressed after bloody fighting, and its leaders were exiled. One significant outcome was that, henceforth, modernising nobles would no longer dominate Lithuanian society. Modernising peasants would take the lead instead.

It was the expectations of these peasants, combined with Western technical progress (including the appearance of railways and electricity), which gave rise to the national reawakening, a clearly modernising movement in society. Indeed, the national revival was rooted in the peasantry.

This process developed under exceptionally difficult circumstances. In 1864 the open Russification of society was begun with the official ban on Lithuanian printed matter in the Latin alphabet. The country responded to rising oppression with the first large wave of emigration. In the second half of the 19th century, almost a third of the population emigrated. In Lithuania Minor, which at the time was ruled by Prussia, activists of the national awakening published in 1883 the first Lithuanian newspaper *Aušra* (The Dawn). The people associated with this newspaper later became the founders of Lithuania's independence. Two of these activists, Jonas Basanavičius and Vincas Kudirka, today are considered to be the fathers of the modern Lithuanian nation.

A key aspect of this movement was the struggle for independent statehood, explicitly formulated during the 1905 revolution in Russia.

If the nobility produced the renowned Romantic poet Adam Mickiewicz in the first half of the 19th century, Lithuania in the late 19th century produced the artist and composer Mikalojus Konstantinas Čiurlionis. His work, quite innovative for his time, became a symbol of Lithuanian culture, and showed that by the early 20th century Lithuania was culturally in tune with the modern nations of Europe and the world.

THE RESTORATION OF STATEHOOD

In 1915, during the First World War, the German army occupied Lithuania. Although the country was administered by the Germans, the Lithuanian Council, composed of the country's intellectual elite, announced the restoration of an independent Lithuania. Bowing to military necessity, however, the Council acknowledged that the country would be forever joined to Germany. This compromise wording was changed on 16 February 1918, however, when the state of Lithuania was declared to be restored without any ties or obligations to a foreign power, and its government was to be elected by a democratically elected parliament.

The 16th of February is today celebrated as the most important state holiday, marking the beginning of a new independent statehood as well as the emergence of a modern society. It proclaimed democratic rule by a democratically elected government, and combined two principles: the restoration of statehood and the right to national self-determination. By contrast, the independence of Finland, Latvia and Estonia, which was proclaimed at about the same time, was also based on the right to self-determination, but not historical statehood.

The conjunction of these two principles soon began having fateful consequences for the country's future. According to historical right, Lithuanians could not imagine themselves without Vilnius, their ancient capital. According to the principle of national self-determination, the right to possess Vilnius was not indisputable: it was a multilingual and ethnically diverse city, inhabited by Jews, Poles, Russians and Belarusians. Only modest numbers of Lithuanians were resident in Vilnius, surrounded by a territory that had lost its Lithuanian identity on account of Polish and Slav influences.

Control over the Vilnius region shifted back and forth during the tumultuous years following the First World War, but wound up in the hands of a Polish military force in 1920. Lithuania never recognised the armed seizure of Vilnius, and the two countries' relations were virtually frozen until the eve of the Second World War.

THE REPUBLIC OF LITHUANIA AND A MODERN SOCIETY

During two decades, from the end of the First World War to the beginning of the Second World War, Lithuania enjoyed a brief period of independence and made good use of it to build the foundations of a modern state. After defending its independence in wars with Poland and the Russian Bolsheviks in the first two years after the declaration of independence, Lithuania set about rebuilding a devasted country and creating new democratic institutions. Although it lost its capital, Vilnius, it did acquire the Klaipėda district and the port of Klaipėda in 1923, thanks to an armed uprising.

Modernisation commenced with the radical land reform of 1922, which over the next 20 years created a modest, but stable economic basis of small farms and co-operative industry. This permitted significant exports of agricultural goods to the West.

However, parliamentary democracy, which had been losing ground in Europe, did not survive in Lithuania, either. A coup on 17 December 1926, brought the Nationalist Party (*tautininkai*) to power, and the authoritarian regime of Antanas Smetona was established. Thus Lithuania also fell prey to what is now known as the crisis of democracy in pre-war Europe. However, the authoritarian regime of Smetona was relatively mild compared to the fascist regimes of Germany and Italy, or totalitarian rule in the neighbouring USSR.

Progress was achieved not only in the economy but in the cultural realm as well. The 1930s were a period of cultural advance and growing contacts with modern European culture. This progress was marked by the emergence of a modern school system and new currents in art and literature, greatly influenced by contemporary Western European trends. Illiteracy, inherited from the Tsarist regime, was largely eliminated.

One symbol of the national revival was the heroism of two Lithuanian-American pilots, Steponas Darius and Stasys Girėnas, who in 1936 crossed the Atlantic Ocean in a single-engine aircraft, but crashed in Germany, not far from their goal in Lithuania. Sporting achievements were also notable: the basketball team won the European championship in 1937, and again in 1939.

Following Poland's occupation of southeast Lithuania and Vilnius, Kaunas became the interim capital. The city developed and grew rapidly and became a true European capital.

The cultural, educational and economic achievements of the 20 years of independence strengthened Lithuania's distinct national identity and helped it to withstand the tragedies of the middle of the 20th century and Soviet rule.

THE LOSSES AND HEROISM OF THE MID-20TH CENTURY

After the outbreak of the Second World War, Lithuania was occupied three times: first by the

LIETUVOS TARYBA
skelbia
Lietuvos nepriklausomybę

Lietuvos Taryba savo posėdyje vasario m. 16 d. 1918 m. vienu balsu nutarė kreiptis: į Rusijos, Vokietijos ir kitų valstybių vyriausybes šiuo pareiškimu:

Lietuvos Taryba, kaipo vienintelė lietuvių tautos atstovybė, remdamos pripažintąja tautų apsisprendimo teise ir lietuvių Vilniaus konferencijos nutarimu rugsėjo m. 18—23 d. 1917 metais, **skelbia atstatanti nepriklausomą, demokratiniais pamatais sutvarkytą Lietuvos valstybę su sostine VILNIUJE** ir tą valstybę atskirianti nuo visų valstybinių ryšių, kurie yra buvę su kitomis tautomis.

Drauge Lietuvos Taryba pareiškia, kad Lietuvos valstybės pamatus ir jos santykius su kitomis valstybėmis privalo galutinai nustatyti kiek galima greičiau sušauktas Steigiamasis Seimas, demokratiniu būdu visų jos gyventojų išrinktas.

Vilnius, vasario 16 d. 1918 m.   Lietuvos Tarybos nariai:

Dr J. Basanavičius, K. Bizauskas, M. Biržiška, S. Banaitis, P. Dovydaitis. St. Kairys, P. Klimas D. Malinauskas, V. Mironas, St. Narutavičius, A. Petrulis, Dr. J. Saulys, K. Saulys. J. Šernas. A. Stulginskis, A Smetona. J. Smilgevičius, J. Staugaitis, J Vailokaitis. J. Vileišis.

*THE NEWSPAPER **LIETUVOS AIDAS** PROCLAIMS THE ACT OF INDEPENDENCE OF 16 FEBRUARY 1918*

USSR in 1940, then by Nazi Germany in 1941, and finally by the USSR again in 1944. The latter occupation was to last over four decades until freedom again in 1990.

This string of tragedies began in August 1939, when Hitler and Stalin concluded a cynical agreement dividing up European territories between the two totalitarian states. According to the 23 August 1939 Molotov-Ribbentrop Pact, and its Amendment of 28 September, Lithuania was to fall into the Soviet zone of influence.

Wasting no time, Moscow soon began applying diplomatic pressure to force consent to the stationing of Soviet troops on Lithuanian territory. The Soviet-Lithuanian Agreement of 10 October 1939 provided the Soviets with the leverage they needed. According to this agreement, Lithuania was to recover its capital, Vilnius, which had been taken over by the USSR from Poland the previous September. On the other hand, Lithuania was compelled to allow Soviet military bases on its territory. In the summer of 1940, when all of Europe was preoccupied with Hitler's military campaign against France, the USSR accused the Lithuanian Government of breaking this agreement. Reacting to alleged Lithuanian provocations, on 14 June 1940, as the world watched German forces marching into Paris, the Soviet Union presented an ultimatum to Lithuania. This included demands to allow the Red Army to enter Lithuania freely. The Government, without protesting, accepted the ultimatum and agreed to the Soviet demands. Lithuania was occupied again.

Stalin wished to give the occupation and annexation the appearance of voluntary membership of the USSR. Therefore, Moscow ordered that staged elections to a national parliament were to be held on 14 July 1940. The parliament then "petitioned" the USSR to incorporate Lithuania.

Although Lithuania became a "Soviet Socialist Republic," in fact its independence was limited to a very narrow autonomy or, to be more precise, purely local responsibilities. Most Western states refused to recognise the country's incorporation into the USSR: its diplomatic representations in the West continued to function even after the occupation. The events of the summer of 1940 inaugurated the era of totalitarian communist rule, which cut off Lithuania from the European traditions that it had cultivated during the independence period. Complete nationalisation, destruction of the private market economy, mass deportations, and Russification were inflicted on Lithuania as the Soviets consolidated their rule. This repressive system was to develop in all its fullness only after the second occupation of 1944.

THE BEGINNING OF THE GERMAN-SOVIET WAR AND THE INSURRECTION OF JUNE 1941

The mass deportations to Siberia and other remote Soviet areas started on 14 June 1941 and lasted a week. Perhaps these actions would have continued had Hitler been slower. Instead, on 22 June 1941, he unleashed the Nazi attack on the Soviet Union. On the same day, the Lithuanian underground resistance launched an uprising, which was centred in Kaunas. To a large extent, this insurrection was a spontaneous reaction to the public shock experienced during the dreadful week of deportations. Since the Sovi-

HUMAN LOSSES IN LITHUANIA IN THE MIDDLE OF THE 20TH CENTURY	
1941 (first six months)	repatriation of Lithuania's Germans (50,000 people); the first mass deportations to the Soviet Union (23,000 people);
1941-1944	Nazi genocide of the Jews (220,000 people);
1943-1944	10,000 people taken to forced labour in Germany; 60,000 people flee to the West;
1945	140,000 inhabitants of the Klaipėda district emigrate;
1945-1946	200,000 Lithuanian Poles deported ("repatriated") to Poland;
1945-1953	mass deportations to Siberia and other eastern parts of the Soviet Union (250,000 people);
1941-1951	about 25,000 resistance fighters and 10,000 Soviet activists and supporters killed.

In this period Lithuania lost almost 30% of its inhabitants.

ets were fleeing from the Germans, some historians do not consider this armed struggle an uprising, but rather a partisan movement. In any case, the armed reaction was not entirely without organisation. The insurgents announced the re-establishment of the Lithuanian state and the formation of an interim government. The Germans arrived in Kaunas, Vilnius and other cities to find already established administrative institutions.

The interim government, over a very brief period, restored the structures that had existed before 14 June 1940 and passed the Law on Denationalisation. However, its activities were hindered by the German military, and subsequently civilian, authorities. That demonstrated that its aims conflicted with German interests. Finally, the government was dissolved by the occupying authorities on 5 August 1941.

Another indication of Lithuanian opposition to German aims was the complete failure of the Nazis to replicate what they were doing in other European countries – recruiting local residents for the combat SS legions. Despite harsh reprisals, the Lithuanian response was one of mass evasion: thousands of men fled to

the woods, some first joining the resistance to the Germans, and later to the returning Soviets.

Nevertheless, the uprising of 1941 and the interim government today remain one of the most controversial subjects in Lithuanian history. Some authors argue that the insurrection may have been more beneficial to the Nazis than to Lithuania itself.

The German occupation became the background for the mass murder of Lithuanian Jews, one of the most tragic events in Lithuanian and Jewish history.* Although Nazi racial policies were at the root of the killings, some Lithuanians assisted the Nazis. Nevertheless, there were many occasions when Lithuanians risked their lives saving Jews. The Yad Vashem Institute in Jerusalem honoured 416 Lithuanians with the designation *Righteous Gentiles* for their heroism in saving Jews from deadly persecution.

A WAR AFTER THE WAR: LITHUANIAN ARMED RESISTANCE TO SOVIET RULE

In the summer of 1944 the second Soviet occupation began. With the Red Army approaching, over 60,000 people fled to

* Described more extensively on page 106

the West. These were mainly educated people and members of the elite who had already suffered in the first Soviet occupation.

Since Stalin not only reshaped the map of Europe but also ordered the relocation of peoples in order to match the new borders, 200,000 Lithuanian Poles were deported en masse to Poland in 1945 and 1946. This was a better fate than that of many Lithuanians who stayed.

In 1945 the mass deportations of Lithuanian families to Siberia and other eastern regions of the USSR resumed, but on a larger scale than in 1941. These deportations continued until the early 1950s, and perhaps would have gone on if not for Stalin's death in 1953. It appears that the phenomenon was not only an action against one class, but a form of mass murder since even poorer people were deported along with wealthier residents.

From 1944, the Soviets implemented mass collectivisation, appropriating land, livestock and other farming assets. This resulted in the establishment of kolkhozes, large farms that were owned de facto by the state. In this way, the old European agricultural tradition, based on private property, was destroyed. Collectivisation was a disaster: the pre-war level of agricultural productivity was matched only in 1960.

The occupation, deportations, collectivisation and terror triggered an armed resistance, even after the War ended. By 1947 it had already developed an organisational structure and covered the whole country. Almost 100,000 people joined the armed resistance, which was scattered around outlying agricultural districts and wooded areas. The resistance was fuelled by hopes that a conflict would erupt between the West and the USSR, and that Western countries, especially the USA, would come to assist the armed resistance. These hopes, however, were in vain.

The resistance movement fought Soviet regular army and specialised NKVD secret police units. From 1949 the armed resistance started to wane; but even under these most desperate conditions it continued to exist until 1953 (the last resistance fighter refused to surrender and shot himself much later, in 1965). Therefore, Lithuania's armed resistance lasted for a decade after the end of the Second World War and was perhaps the longest in Europe. It can rightly be called "a war after the war." One of its effects was a lower level of Soviet colonisation (as compared with other Soviet republics) on account of the obvious security concerns. Resistance leaders, most of whom perished, are honoured in contemporary Lithuania.

UNDER COMMUNIST RULE

After crushing the armed resistance, the USSR created a totalitarian system comparable to that of the ancient Eastern despotic states. The planned, or perhaps more precisely, command economy; one-party rule; mass surveillance and terror carried out by the NKVD and subsequently the KGB; the compulsory adherence to Marxist-Leninist ideology; the quasi-religious cult of the "great leaders", Lenin, Stalin, Khrushchev and Brezhnev: these were some of the features of the political system that was forcibly established in Lithuania.

After Stalin's death a partial liberalisation of the system followed, known as the Khrushchev thaw. It was during this relative liberalisation that ethnic Russians in the Communist Party were replaced by some non-Russian members.

Thus the Lithuanian party *nomenklatūra*, tolerant of the country's language and culture, took root. Although the liberali-

sation only lasted until the end of the 1960s, it to some extent allowed a new generation to carry out valuable artistic and scientific work and to use technological developments for the public good. This was especially visible with respect to Lithuanian roads, some of which matched European standards even during the Soviet era. It was this same generation which would later become the main force behind Lithuania's national rebirth. These same individuals took the risk of disaffiliating the Lithuanian Communist Party from the Communist Party of the Soviet Union, the first such separation in the postwar era.

The 1970s was a period that was subsequently called stagnation by Soviet writers. The Soviet economy increasingly fell behind the economies of the West. At first glance, Lithuania seemed to be making some progress. However, much of what was seen as industrial growth relied too much on extensive use of raw materials and labour and too little on technical innovation and labour rationalisation.

In the latter years of Soviet rule, several large chemical plants such as the Mažeikiai Oil Refinery and the Ignalina Nuclear Power Plant were built. Moscow's motivation seemed at least partly to be political. It sought to make the Lithuanian economy dependent on Soviet raw materials and markets, and to encourage a large influx of labour from outlying Soviet regions.

During this period the country's resistance to the communist system was renewed. The dissident movement received encouragement from the Prague Spring. Lithuania's reaction to it was reflected in the 1972 events in Kaunas: Romas Kalanta's self-immolation provoked protests by young people, which predictably were suppressed by the KGB.

The dissident movement manifested itself in two main forms: the struggle for the rights of Catholics (mainly through the underground publication *Chronicle of the Catholic Church*) and a movement that concentrated on the protection of human rights (the Helsinki Group, which appeared in 1976).

On another level, the country expressed its national determination through sports competitions, especially basketball. The powerful Kaunas Žalgiris basketball team, fortified by Arvydas Sabonis, successfully challenged the best that Soviet basketball had to offer. Žalgiris victories over Moscow's CSKA team had ideological overtones since the latter was formed from Soviet army personnel. Žalgiris-CSKA encounters in USSR tournament finals between 1982 and 1987 are considered to some extent to have stimulated the country's national reawakening several years later.

THE SINGING REVOLUTION AND THE RESTORATION OF INDEPENDENCE

In 1985 the Soviet government, unable to compete economically with the West, was forced to consider change. Gorbachev's perestroika had a crucial, and unexpected, impact on events in Lithuania.

The political liberalisation of the Gorbachev years very quickly was transformed into political ferment. The rebirth, also called the Singing Revolution because so many of the popular manifestations were accompanied by folk songs, received political direction from the Sąjūdis movement, which was founded on 3 June 1988. During that summer, Sąjūdis organised meetings that brought together hundreds of thousands of people. This was a turning point in modern Lithuanian history.

Sąjūdis' first congress convened on 22 and 23 October 1988. From that moment, Sąjūdis began acting as an organised opposition

LITHUANIAN CITIZENS GUARDING THE SUPREME COUNCIL AGAINST A POSSIBLE ATTACK, JANUARY 1991

to the Communist Party. The next year, Sąjūdis participated in elections to the highest body of the Soviet administration, the Congress of People's Deputies. This was the first time in the USSR's modern history when an organised parliamentary opposition emerged, formed chiefly of delegates from the Baltic states.

In order to demonstrate to Moscow the grass-roots nature and solidarity of the rebirth, its leadership decided to hold a mass protest coinciding with the 50th anniversary (23 August 1989) of the Molotov-Ribbentrop Pact. Sąjūdis, together with analogous Estonian and Latvian groups, organised the largest ever mass protest in the Baltic states. About two million people linked hands in a human chain that stretched 650 kilometres from Vilnius to Tallinn.

On 24 February 1990, Sąjūdis won 106 seats out of a total of 141 in the local Supreme Council elections. This council, which was later renamed the Reconstituent Seimas, announced

the reestablishment of Lithuania's independence on 11 March 1990.

Moscow refused to accept the outcome of this vote. Independence was met by an economic blockade, and on 13 January 1991, when the world's attention was focused on the conflict with Iraq in the Persian Gulf, Moscow attempted to overthrow Lithuania's legitimate Government. The crackdown, carried out by armed force against unarmed citizens, resulted in 14 dead and hundreds injured. Only the mass peaceful resistance of the people prevented the Soviet army from storming the parliament building. It later became clear that the January events in Vilnius were a dress rehearsal for the failed Moscow putsch in August 1991.

Only after the coup failed was the Republic of Lithuania recognised by most states (an exception was the solitary stance of Iceland, which recognised Lithuania as early as February 1991). On 17 September 1991, Lithuania joined the United Nations, and on 31 August 1993, Soviet troops were finally withdrawn.

LITHUANIAN JEWRY

The history of Jews in Lithuania begins in the 14th century after Grand Duke Gediminas invited people "of all nations and faiths" to come to Lithuania to build his new capital city, Vilnius. The Grand Duchy of Lithuania seemed an island of tolerance in a sea of antisemitism, and Jews under the grand dukes were granted rights they did not have in many other parts of Europe, including rights to property and freedom of religion. Vilnius, known to the Jewish community as Vilna, came to be called The Jerusalem of Lithuania. Among the reasons for this designation was that at one time, according to legend, there were 333 Vilnius Jews who were able to memorize the entire Talmud.

Although Lithuania was not as densely populated by Jews as other countries in Eastern Europe, it was a leading centre of Jewish culture and learning. By the 18th century, Vilnius was the world centre of Talmudic scholarship, and had the largest number of Talmudic scholars in the world. The most famous of them, Eliyahu ben-Shlomo Zalman (1720-1797), known as the Gaon of Vilna, is one of the most prominent figures of Jewish history in Lithuania. Today his achievements are officially remembered by a memorial, which was unveiled on the occasion of the 200th anniversary of his death. The memorial is located on Gaon Street, in the former Jewish quarter of Vilnius.

After Lithuania was annexed by Tsarist Russia in 1795, Jews in Lithuania lived under better conditions than their coreligionists in Russia. Lithuania was one of the few regions included in the so-called Pale of Settlement, where Jewish culture was officially allowed to develop. Jewish printing presses were only permitted in two cities in the Tsarist empire: Kiev and Vilnius. The very first book published in modern Hebrew, *The Love of Zion* (1855), was written and published by Abraham Mapu in Lithuania.

Many famous Jews called Lithuania their home. Today Jerusalem and Tel Aviv have streets named after the outstanding Jewish linguist, the founder of modern Hebrew, Eliezer Ben-Jehuda (1858-1923), who was born in Lithuania.

Lithuania and Vilnius are closely associated with leading figures of modern Israeli history, such as Levi Eshkol, Israel's third prime minister. Eshkol studied in a Hebrew school in Vilnius. The fifth prime minister of Israel, Menachem Begin, started his long road to Siberian exile in Vilnius, where he was arrested by Soviet police. Ehud Barak, recently elected Israeli Prime Minister, also has Lithuanian roots: his father was born near Panevėžys.

Significant events in the history of Zionism were associated with Lithuania, although the anti-Zionist Jewish socialist organisation *Bund* was also founded in Vilnius. The foremost leader of the *Bund*, Aaron Kremer, is buried in the Lithuanian capital. In 1887, the second congress of the movement *Hovevei Zion* (The Lovers of Zion), which was the predecessor of the World Zionist Organisation, was held in Druskininkai. Vilnius served in 1902 as an important conference venue for the founders of the religious Zionist party *Mizrachi.*

Lithuania was also the birthplace of many outstanding Zionist personalities, such as David Wolffsohn, the second president of the World Zionist Organisation; Leo Motzkin, one of its leading figures; and Moshe Leib Lilienblum, one of the founders of *Hovevei Zion.*

The founder of Zionism, Theodore Herzl, visited Vilnius in 1903. To commemorate this event a memorial plaque was unveiled in the Old Town of Vilnius in 1998.

Many of this century's renowned Jewish artists and musicians resided in Lithuania for significant periods of their lives. The sculptor Jacques Lipchitz, the violinist Jascha Heifitz, the landscape artist Isaac Levitan, and the philosopher Emmanuel Levinas all were born and studied in Lithuania.

When Lithuania regained its independence in 1918, the repressive atmosphere that had characterised Russian rule changed significantly. In many Jewish histories of the period, inter-war Lithuania is referred to as their Golden Age. According to Walter Lacquer's *A History of Zionism*, "...the position of the Jewish minority was better than at any time before or since. They enjoyed full minority rights until 1924, and there was a minister for Jewish Affairs in Lithuania."

Paul Johnson, writing in his *A History of the Jews*, noted that: "In Lithuania, which the Soviets did not dare annex until 1939 [sic], these minority guarantees worked well, and the large Jewish community there was perhaps the most contented in Eastern Europe between the wars."

107

In 1925, the Jewish Science Institute, or JIVO (Jiddisher Visinschlaftlecher Institut), was founded in Vilnius. Vilnius was chosen instead of New York and Warsaw as the location of this institution, which included among its board members Albert Einstein and Sigmund Freud.

After the Soviet occupation of Lithuania in 1940, however, the situation changed abruptly. The German invasion of the Soviet Union in June 1941 set the stage for the Nazis' mass murder of Lithuanian Jewry. The killings reached a peak in August and September 1941: during these months over 70,000 Jews were murdered, which meant that in the provinces almost every Jew was killed. The survivors were in the Vilnius, Kaunas and Šiauliai ghettos. By the autumn of that year, however, mass murders were also being carried out in the ghettos.

In Kaunas, 10,000 Jews were shot on 28 and 29 October 1941. At the end of 1941 approximately 40,000 Jews remained in the ghettos; they were also murdered, although at a slower pace. The Vilnius ghetto was completely liquidated on 23 September 1943.

Although the chief force behind these crimes was the Nazi regime, some Lithuanians were involved. At the same time, many other Lithuanians subjected themselves to grave risk by sheltering Jews from the killings.

Thus, Lithuania, home to the Jerusalem of Lithuania, became the site of a catastrophe for the Jewish people. During the years 1941 to 1944, approximately 220,000 Lithuanian Jews were brutally murdered, 94% of the country's Jewish population. The Holocaust in Lithuania is one of the most tragic episodes in Lithuanian and Jewish history.

After the Second World War the number of Jews living in Lithuania recovered slightly, reaching a peak of 16,000 in 1959.

The creation of the State of Israel encouraged the emigration of Jews from the Soviet Union, and their struggle for the right to emigrate gained new momentum after 1967. Soviet police repressed Zionist activity in Lithuania and all over the Soviet Union. From 1948 to 1950, the Soviets closed down Jewish community and educational institutions. Nevertheless, thousands of Lithuanian Jews took the opportunity that relaxed Soviet emigration policies gave them to escape the repressive Soviet regime and move to Israel and the West.

Today there are only 6,000 Jews living in Lithuania, a small but very active community. A Jewish gymnasium exists in Vilnius, and scores of Jewish cultural events are held each year, many of which commemorate the grand, and tragic, centuries of the Lithuanian Jewish heritage.

R` ELIYAHU THE GAON OF VILNA (1720-1797)

THE POLES
AND LITHUANIA

In the first half of the 19th century, Vilnius became the most important centre of Polish Romanticism. Its most outstanding representative was Adam Mickiewicz, sometimes referred to as medieval Lithuania's bard. Mickiewicz (known in Lithuanian as Adomas Mickevičius) participated in organising an anti-Tsar-ist student society called the *filomatai* during his studies at Vilnius University. His underground activities earned him imprisonment and later exile in Russia. Following Russian exile, Mickiewicz, like other Polish-Lithuanian political activists, found refuge in Paris. Mickiewicz's epic poems *Gražyna* and *Konrad Wallenrod* glorified the Lithuanians' struggles against the Teutonic Order, and

Pan Tadeusz proclaimed the idea of national liberation from the Russian Empire.

Several other prominent writers of the Polish Romantic tradition studied and matured as artists in Lithuania, including Juliusz Słowacki, Władysław Syrokomla and Józef Ignac Kraszewski. Their writings relied extensively on a mixture of Lithuanian history, mythology and folklore.

These, and many other celebrated Polish artists, considered themselves Poles in terms of citizenship, but Lithuanians by origin.

One of the best-known such Lithuanian Poles in the world of politics is undoubtedly Józef Piłsudski (1867-1935), Poland's most influential statesman and head of state in the pre-war era. In his early youth Piłsudski took an active part in the pre-First

Konrad Wallenrod.

POWIEŚĆ HISTORYCZNA

z

DZIEJÓW LITEWSKICH I PRUSKICH

PRZEZ

Adama Mickiewicza.

> *Dovete adunque sapere come sono due generazioni da combattere... bisogna essere volpe e leone.*

PETERSBURG.
DRUKIEM KAROLA KRAYA.
1828.

MICKIEWICZ'S ROMANTIC ACCOUNTS OF LITHUANIA'S STRUGGLE AGAINST THE TEUTONIC ORDER INSPIRED GENERATIONS OF POLES

World War independence movement. During this war he was one of the founders of the Polish Legions.

Piłsudski believed in a restored Polish-Lithuanian union, in which Lithuania and Belarus would be bound to Poland in a federation. This, he thought, would solve the complicated border problems plaguing Lithuanian-Polish relations and the question of Vilnius, which was so dear to him. Piłsudski's heart is buried in *Rasų* cemetery in Vilnius. This monument to Piłsudski is frequently honoured by Polish dignitaries on official visits to Lithuania.

Piłsudski's vision was shared by Michał Römer (1880-1945), a prominent jurisprudence expert and rector of Vytautas Magnus University in Kaunas. Römer dreamed of and attempted to implement in practice the concept of a common homeland of Lithuanians, Belarusians, Poles and Lithuanian Jews in a restored Grand Duchy of Lithuania.

Stanisław Narutowicz (1862-1932), a political activist from Samogitia (Žemaitija, or the western part of Lithuania), became an energetic spokesman for this idea. Nevertheless, Narutowicz (Stanislovas Narutavičius) became one of the signatories of the Lithuanian Declaration of Independence of 16 February 1918, the only Pole to have signed this document. His brother, Gabriel Narutowicz, taught at Zürich, later returning to Poland to serve as foreign minister and then as Poland's first president after the First World War.

In the world of music, Polish Lithuanians take pride in Stanisław Moniuszko (1819-1872). Moniuszko was born near Minsk, but he and his musical work were closely associated with Vilnius for a good part of his life. He and Frederic Chopin were among the chief representatives of Polish Romantic music. Moniuszko composed the opera *Halka*, and was one of the founders of Polish opera.

The sculptor Antoni Wiwulski (1877-1919) created the Grünwald Monument in Kraków and the Three Crosses Monument in Vilnius. Wiwulski was also a renowned architect, having designed the Sacred Heart Church in Vilnius.

The contemporary writer and poet Czesław Miłosz was born in Lithuania and was closely associated with the Żagary group of poets in Vilnius during the 1930s. Miłosz was awarded the Nobel Prize for Literature. He now resides in the USA, and his works have been published in many languages.

112

LITHUANIA IN THE LIVES OF RUSSIAN NOTABLES

A number of well-known Russian writers, artists, painters and historical figures had important ties with Lithuania. Dovmont, the medieval Duke of Pskov who was canonised by the Orthodox Church (Saint Timofey), in reality was a Lithuanian named Daumantas.

Tsar Peter the Great christened Alexander Pushkin's great-grandfather in Vilnius. And the youngest son of the great Russian poet, Grigory Pushkin (1835-1905), lived out the last six years of his life and was buried in a suburb of Vilnius, Markučiai.

The famous Russian reform statesman, Piotr Stolypin, also studied in Vilnius. Stolypin spent his vacations at his father's estate near the central Lithuanian town of Kėdainiai. After completing his university studies, the young Stolypin served as the chairman of the Kaunas district court, during which time he devoted himself to social work, founding schools for peasant children. When he became Russian prime minister he continued spending his summers at his father's estate at Kalnaberžė. This is where Stolypin developed his ideas on reforming the Russian Empire's agricultural system.

Aleksey Lvov (1798-1870), a violinist and composer of the Russian national anthem, *God Save the Tsar*, lies buried at the Pažaislis Monastery near Kaunas. The sculptor Mark Antokolsky (1843-1902) spent his childhood in Vilnius. The painter and graphic artist Mstislav Dobuzhinsky studied at a gymnasium in Vilnius and often visited the city in later years. From 1924 to 1939, he lived and painted in Kaunas. Dobuzhinsky's ancestors originated from the village of Dabužiai.

From 1905 to 1911, Mikhail Bakhtin studied at a secondary school in Vilnius. He was a philologist and philosopher of world renown.

From 1928 until the outbreak of the Second World War, Lev Karsavin, a prominent historian of culture and philosopher, taught at the University of Kaunas. Following the end of the war, Karsavin, like many other Russian cultural figures in Lithuania, was subject to official persecution.

The world-renowned bass soloist Fyodor Shaliapin performed in Lithuania in 1895, 1910 and 1934. Shaliapin was a close associate of the Lithuanian tenor Kipras Petrauskas, with whom he shared the opera stage on a number of occasions. One of

113

Russia's most outstanding contemporary prose writers, Konstantin Vorobyov, spent virtually his entire life in Lithuania and died in Vilnius in 1975.

The poet Konstantin Balmont (1867-1943) and the prose writer and Nobel laureate Ivan Bunin (1870-1953) had Lithuanian roots. The ancestors of Mstislav Rostropovich, the renowned cellist, lived in Lithuania. Maya Pliseckaya, the prima ballerina, and her husband, Rodyon Shchedrin, one of Russia's best-known contemporary composers, often

VILNIUS ENVIRONS. RIBIŠKĖS. 1848.
ALPHONSE BICHEBOIS AND VICTOR ADAM

114

vacation in their summer villa in the picturesque Trakai lake district. Both of them were granted Lithuanian citizenship for their contribution to Lithuania's musical life.

Lithuania's relatively liberal atmosphere stimulated the development of the talents of two premier jazz musicians, Vladimir Tarasov from Archangelsk and Vladimir Chekasin from Sverdlovsk. They started the Ganelin-Tarasov-Chekasin jazz trio, which was the only established jazz musical group in the USSR.

THE STATE

The Constitution of the Republic of Lithuania, which defines the nation's political, economic and legal systems, was approved in 1992 by popular referendum. Article One affirms the fundamental constitutional principle of statehood: that Lithuania is an independent and democratic republic. This principle was endorsed by more than three quarters of all Lithua-

nian citizens with suffrage rights in a democratic vote on 9 February 1991. According to the Constitution, sovereignty is vested in the people. The territory of the state is whole and complete and cannot be divided.

The powers of the state are exercised by the Seimas (parliament), the President of the Republic, the Government and the judiciary. Central issues concerning the state and the people are decided by referendum.

THE PRESIDENT'S OFFICE

In practice, the Government, with its constituent ministries, exercises broad authority over day-to-day affairs, particularly in the economic realm.

The President, assisted by his staff of advisors, concerns himself with broad policy questions, particularly in the security and foreign affairs fields. The prestige of the Office of the President lends the incumbent considerable moral authority; the President's expressed views on matters of state carry great weight.

Although the Seimas is mainly involved in the work of passing and amending legislation, it also has significant oversight authority over implementation of its laws by the Government and other official bodies. The parliament's role in forming and passing the budget is, of course, of key importance to the governing of the country. In practice, the leadership of the Seimas is intimately involved in the policy making process, consulting extensively with the Government and the President on major issues.

Political observers sometimes refer to Lithuania as a semi-parliamentary republic in which the the Seimas, President and Government seek consensus through a continuous process of consultation and coordination.

117

The articles of the Constitution dealing with the relationship between the individual and the state ensure the inviolability of personal freedom, privacy, property and domicile. Freedom of thought, conscience and religion cannot be restricted. Citizens have the right to participate in the running of the state both directly or through their democratically elected representatives. Ethnic minorities enjoy the right to foster their language, culture and customs. Any person whose constitutional rights are violated has the right to appeal through the courts.

Lithuania's economy is based on the right to private ownership, freedom of individual economic activity, and personal initiative. The Republic of Lithuania has exclusive ownership rights to the air space over its territory, its continental shelf, and the economic zone in the Baltic Sea. Mineral rights, inland waters, forests, parks, roads, and historical, archaeological and cultural facilities belong to the state.

In order to amend or append the Constitution, a proposal must be submitted to the Seimas (parliament) by either at least a quarter of the members of the Seimas, or by a minimum of 300,000 voters. Article One of the Constitution, which states that Lithuania is an independent democratic republic, may only be amended by a referendum in which at least three quarters of the electorate vote in favour.

Amendments to other articles must be debated and approved by the Seimas twice (there must be a period of at least three months between each vote). Bills regarding constitutional amendments are considered to have passed the Seimas if, in each of the votes, at least two thirds of all the members of the Seimas vote in favour.

Lithuania's Constitution includes the Act on the Non-Alignment of the Republic of Lithuania to Post-Soviet Eastern Alliances.

THE SEIMAS

The Lithuanian parliament is the key institution of national representation and legislation of the state. The Seimas consists of 141 members, who are elected for a four-year term on the basis of universal, equal and direct suffrage by secret ballot. Any citizen who is not bound by an oath or pledge to a foreign state, and who, on the day of the election, is 25 years of age or over and resides permanently in Lithuania, may be elected a member of the Seimas. Newly elected members receive the right to represent the people after taking an oath of loyalty in the Seimas.

The Seimas, inter alia, considers and enacts amendments to the Constitution; enacts laws; announces presidential elections; forms state institutions according to the law, and appoints and dismisses their heads; approves or rejects the candidature of the Prime Minister proposed by the President; considers the Government programme submitted by the Prime Minister and decides upon its approval or rejection; supervises the Government, and may pass a vote of no-confidence in the Prime Minister or his ministers; appoints judges and chairmen of the Constitutional Court and the Supreme Court; appoints and dismisses the State Controller and the Chairman of the Board of the Bank of Lithuania; convenes the General Electoral Commission and calls elections; approves the state budget and supervises its implementation; ratifies and denounces international treaties, and debates other issues of foreign policy; regulates the administrative division of the country; grants amnesty; imposes direct administration and martial law, declares a state of emergency, announces conscription, and passes decisions to use the armed forces.

The first national elections following the restoration of independence were held in 1992. They were won by the Lithuanian Democratic Labour Party. Four years later, the Homeland Union (Lithuanian Conservatives) won a parliamentary majority.

Members of the current Seimas belong to seven factions. Bills are initially considered, and sometimes even drafted by, 13 standing committees. Seven commissions have been established. Seimas organisational issues are decided by the Board of the Seimas, which consists of the Chairman, his four deputies and the Chancellor.

The Seimas' work is led by its Chairman (at present Prof. Vytautas Landsbergis). His functions may be carried out by deputy chairmen on his request.

The sittings of the Seimas are open to the public.

The Seimas participates in the activities of international and European institutions of inter-parliamentary co-operation. The Baltic Assembly, established in 1991, is of special importance for the co-operation of the Baltic states and their integration into the European Union. In order to develop a partnership between Lithuania and Poland and encourage good neighbourliness, the Assembly of Lithuanian and Polish Members of Parliament has been established.

PRESIDENT VALDAS ADAMKUS AND US PRESIDENT BILL CLINTON, WASHINGTON, D.C., OCTOBER, 1998

THE PRESIDENT
OF THE REPUBLIC

The President of the Republic of Lithuania is the head of state. Any person who is a Lithuanian citizen by birth, who has lived in Lithuania for at least the previous three years, and who has reached 40 years of age prior to the day of election to the presidency may be elected President. A person may not be elected President for more than two consecutive terms.

The President's functions are, inter alia, as follows: he or she rules on major foreign policy issues and, together with the Gov-ernment, implements foreign policy; signs international treaties and submits them to the Seimas for ratification; appoints and re-calls, on the Government's recom-mendation, diplomatic repre-sentatives to foreign states and in-ternational organisations; ap-points and dismisses, on the Seimas' approval, the Prime Min-ister; proposes to the Seimas can-didates as Supreme Court judges, State Controller and the Chair-man of the Board of the Bank of Lithuania; appoints and dismisses the head of the armed forces and the head of the security service; grants amnesty; signs and prom-ulgates laws enacted by the Seimas.

The President may announce pre-term elections to the Seimas if, among other things, the latter fails to pass a decision on the Government's new programme within 30 days, or at the suggestion of the Government, if the Seimas passes a vote of no-confidence in the Government.

The President is also Commander-in-Chief of the Armed Forces and heads the State Defence Council.

In 1993 Algirdas Brazauskas was elected by direct popular vote as Lithuania's first president since the restoration of independence. The 1998 presidential election was won by Valdas Adamkus, who had previously lived abroad and served as Administrator of the Fifth Region (Mid-West) of the US Environmental Protection Agency.

THE GOVERNMENT

The Government of the Republic of Lithuania is the highest executive body. It is made up of the Prime Minister and 14 ministers.

The Prime Minister is, with the Seimas' approval, appointed or dismissed by the President. The ministers are appointed by the President on their nomination by the Prime Minister. A new Government is empowered to act after the Seimas approves its programme by majority vote. On taking up their duties, the Prime Minister and ministers take an oath in the Seimas to be loyal to the Republic of Lithuania and to honour its Constitution and laws.

The Government carries out the administration of the state by issuing directives that must be passed by a majority vote of all ministers. The Government is responsible for its actions to the Seimas.

At the request of the Seimas, the Government or individual ministers must give an account of their activities to the Seimas. When more than half the ministers are changed, the Government must be re-invested with authority by the Seimas; otherwise the Government must resign. A minister must resign if more than half the Seimas members express, in a secret ballot, a lack of confidence in him or her. The resignation of the Government or its ministers must be accepted by the President.

The following ministries function in the Republic of Lithuania: Environment; Finance; Defence; Culture; Social Security and Employment; Transport; Health; Education and Science; Justice; Economy; Foreign Affairs; Public Administration Reforms and Local Authorities; Internal Affairs and Agriculture.

The administration of the Prime Minister's Office is headed by the Chancellor.

PRIME MINISTER ROLANDAS PAKSAS (RIGHT) AND ROLAND KOCH, CHAIRMAN OF THE BUNDESRAT OF THE FEDERAL REPUBLIC OF GERMANY AND PRIME MINISTER OF THE FEDERAL STATE OF HESSEN, IN VILNIUS, JULY 1999

The Government has the right to request the President to announce pre-term elections if the Seimas expresses no-confidence in the Government.

When more than half the ministers are changed or a new President is elected, the Government must return its powers. In that case the President appoints the Government to act until it receives renewed powers from the Seimas or a new Government is formed.

The Government must resign if the Seimas rejects on two consecutive occasions the Government's programme; when a majority of Seimas members expresses a lack of confidence in the Government or the Prime Minister in a secret vote; when the Prime Minister resigns or dies or after a new Seimas is elected. The Government may resign at the Prime Minister's suggestion by issuing a Government decree.

COURTS

Lithuanian law is based on European law. The Ministry of Justice deals with the harmonisation of legislation with European Union law, within the framework of judicial cooperation in civil and criminal matters. After Lithuania joined the Council of Europe in 1993, key legal instruments regarding human rights, as well as most relevant conventions on criminal law, have been acceded to and ratified. In 1998 Lithuania abolished capital punishment.

Lithuania's judicial system was established by Article Nine of the Constitution, and the Law on Courts which was passed in 1994. Justice is applied by the courts only. Courts and judges are independent, and judges' decisions are based on the law.

In all courts, cases are heard in public. A court hearing may be held in camera only in exceptional cases, in order to protect a person's or family's privacy, or a state, professional or commercial secret.

The following courts operate in Lithuania: the Supreme Court, the Court of Appeal, regional, district and administrative courts.

The Constitution provides for the establishment of special courts, should the need arise, in order to investigate specific kinds of cases. During peacetime, no courts with special powers may be established.

The district courts investigate civil, criminal and administrative cases, and pass sentences. There are currently 54 district courts.

The regional courts investigate civil and criminal cases, and hear appeals against decisions made by district courts. There are five regional courts.

The Court of Appeal hears appeals against decisions made by regional courts. It also investigates cases that come under its jurisdiction under national law.

The Supreme Court is the only institution that can hear an appeal against a court's decision which has already come into force. Cases are investigated by a collegium consisting of three judges, or its extended form consisting of seven judges, or by a plenary session of the court.

The Senate of the Supreme Court, consisting of the Chairman, the chairmen of its divisions and other judges of the court, analyses the practice of courts in hearing cases, and approves the summary of court practice announced in a special bulletin.

A system of administrative courts has been established. These courts address issues related to administrative law and disputes in the area of public administration.

In order to represent and protect the professional interests of the judges of all courts, including the Constitutional Court, the Association of Judges was established in 1993. It has almost 400 members. The Lithuanian Association of Judges is a member of the International Organisation of Judges.

In order to register mortgaged property, the Hypothec Registry was established in 1996. It is the youngest and most modern state registry in Eastern and Central Europe.

The directory of court advocates lists over 750 members. There are offices in every town and district centre that has a court. The Court Advocates' Board is the main institution that organises and co-ordinates their activities.

As early as the 13th century there were notary services in Lithuania. According to the Lithuanian Statute of 1588, court secretaries also carried out notarial duties. Modern notarial practice is based on the 1992 Notary Law. There are more than 130 notary offices across the country.

The Prosecutor's Office is an independent government agency. All prosecutors and other officials in the Prosecutor's Office belong to a single centralised system.

The Constitutional Court investigates whether laws and other acts passed by the Seimas and approved by the President and the Government do not contravene the Constitution or other laws. The right to appeal to the Constitutional Court is held by the Government, no less than one fifth of all members of the Seimas, and the courts. The Seimas may request a ruling from the Constitutional Court. The President may request a ruling concerning elections to the Seimas and international agreements. The decisions of the Constitutional Court are final and not subject to appeal.

The Constitutional Court consists of nine judges, who are nominated for nine years each and for a single term only. Every three years, the court is renewed by one third.

Special working groups have been established at the Ministry of Justice to prepare new amendments to the criminal code, codes of penal procedure, execution of punishments, civil matters (commercial and family issues), civil lawsuits, and violations of administrative law. All these drafts are to be turned into bills and passed by the year 2000.

LOCAL GOVERNMENT

Local government has old traditions in Lithuania. Its origins can be traced to the Middle Ages, during which Lithuanian towns

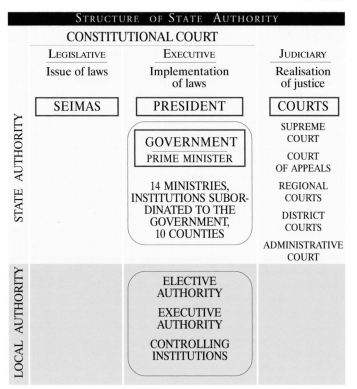

STRUCTURE OF STATE AUTHORITY

CONSTITUTIONAL COURT

LEGISLATIVE	EXECUTIVE	JUDICIARY
Issue of laws	Implementation of laws	Realisation of justice

STATE AUTHORITY

| SEIMAS | PRESIDENT | COURTS |

GOVERNMENT
PRIME MINISTER

14 MINISTRIES, INSTITUTIONS SUBORDINATED TO THE GOVERNMENT, 10 COUNTIES

SUPREME COURT

COURT OF APPEALS

REGIONAL COURTS

DISTRICT COURTS

ADMINISTRATIVE COURT

LOCAL AUTHORITY

ELECTIVE AUTHORITY

EXECUTIVE AUTHORITY

CONTROLLING INSTITUTIONS

received Magdeburg and Kulm Rights. Local parliaments, called *seimeliai*, also began functioning in the 16th century.

Magdeburg Rights recognised the right of the inhabitants of a city to have local government and an independent court and to regulate crafts and trade. The first town to receive Magdeburg Rights in Lithuania was Vilnius (1387). Kulm Rights gave cities and towns the right to organise municipal government. The *seimeliai* existed from 1566 to 1803, and were a local district authority of the Grand Duchy of Lithuania: they consisted of, and were elected by, the nobility.

Pre-war Lithuania's Law on Local Government provided for three types of local government: town, district and village. Of these village councils proved to be the focal point of local authority.

During the Soviet era, the Councils of Deputies of Working People had no genuine power since their decisions conformed to orders issued by local Communist Party bodies or higher authorities.

After 1990, this state of affairs changed as the authorities began introducing administrative decentralisation. The Law on Local Government of 1994 stipulated that "local rule and the exercise of de facto power is a right granted by the Constitution and laws of the Republic of Lithuania." Lithuania was divided into two basic administrative units: county and district.

Counties, the higher administrative units, execute the national Government's regional policies. These administrative units have overall responsibility for land and land reform. Counties monitor the work of districts and lower-level authorities.

Lithuania is divided administratively into ten counties, whose administrative centres are located in the major towns: Alytus, Kaunas, Klaipėda, Marijampolė, Panevėžys, Šiauliai, Tauragė, Telšiai, Utena and Vilnius (county boundaries are set forth in the map provided at the end of this book).

Districts, the lower administrative units, are governed by elected bodies. The right of self-rule is currently enjoyed by 12 larger towns and 44 districts. The districts are sub-divided into 449 village councils.

The right of self-rule is realised through district councils. People residing in districts elect their councils for a period of three years. The councils make the major local decisions, although some district issues may also be addressed by local executive bodies, the mayor or the board.

Local government bodies (as distinct from the county administrations) exercise autonomous authority over the following areas: public utilities, housing, streets, mass transit and zoning. Local government authorities are also empowered to implement a variety of national Government functions, including the recording of civil records, the registration of enterprises, the provision of secondary health care, the management of national nature preserves, the organisation of local government police forces as well as civil and fire safety services. Local government is charged with organising education and social policies.

During the 1997 district council elections, majorities were secured by the Homeland Union (Lithuanian Conservatives) in most of Lithuania. The Democratic Labour Party came in second, followed by the Christian Democratic Party and the Social Democratic Party.

126

FOREIGN AFFAIRS AND SECURITY POLICY

The principal goal of Lithuania's foreign policy is to create a secure environment for the country and its people, to safeguard the continuity of statehood and to ensure future development and prosperity. Lithuania's foreign policy is based on three major objectives: full membership in the European Union (EU), full membership in NATO and the maintenance of good relations with neighbouring states.

THE EUROPEAN UNION

Membership in the European Union is a strategic objective of Lithuania's foreign and domestic policy. This will require fundamental changes in all areas of life. EU membership is indispensable to Lithuania in order to strengthen the country's European identity and to promote economic development. The 50-year Soviet annexation is a vivid reminder that in order to survive and secure its cultural and national identity, Lithuania needs active participation in a wider European framework.

Lithuania applied for EU membership on 8 December 1995. The legal context and background to its integration into the EU consist of the following three main agreements with the EC(EU):

The Agreement on Economic, Commercial and Trade Co-Operation between the EC and Lithuania was signed on 11 May 1992. It established relations and laid the foundations for co-operation between the EC and Lithuania. A joint declaration by the European Community and the Baltic states on political dialogue opened the way to political co-operation;

The Agreement on Free Trade and Trade-Related Matters was concluded on 18 July 1994. It formed an integral part of the Europe (Association) Agreement, and covered trade, state aid, intellectual property rights and public procurement rules;

The Europe Agreement (signed on 12 June 1995 and entered into force on 1 February 1998) established an association between the European Union and its member states, and Lithuania. It recognises Lithuania's goal to become an EU member and paves the way for Lithuania's participation in the EU's Pre-Accession Strategy for the Associate Countries of Central and Eastern Europe. It also upgrades the political dialogue and lays down rules for liberalising the movement of people, goods and services, and co-operation in the spheres of law approximation, finance, environment and culture.

The Europe Agreement also laid down the institutional framework for implementation and management of all areas of Lithuanian-EU relations. It consists of the so called association institutions, namely, Association Council, Association Committee and Sub-committees. The Association Council operates at the ministerial level and examines the overall status of relations and provides the opportunity to review Lithuania's progress in preparing for accession. The Association Committee functions at a senior official level, provides for in-depth discussion of and finds solutions to issues arising under the Agreement. Sub-committees examine questions at a technical level.

Since the entry into force of the European Agreement, two Council, two Committee meeting, and 14 Sub-committee meetings were held. The latest Association Council, held on 22 February 1999 in Luxembourg, noted that "after one year of functioning of the Europe Agreement, the association mechanisms have reached their cruising speed and allow for fruitful co-operation between Lithuania and the European Union.". Whereas the second Association Committee meeting (held in Vilnius on 18 June 1999) focused on Lithuania's preparation for accession and the implementation of the Accession Partnership, which sets priorities for these preparations in economic reform, internal market, energy policy, public administration reform, justice and home affairs, environment and agriculture. An updated EU-Lithuania Accession Partnership will be adopted by the end of 1999.

Lithuanian-EU dialogue is also shaped by an important parliamentary channel, the Lithuania-EU Joint Parliamentary Committee. It has held four meetings in which Lithuania's accession progress was analysed.

The Governmental European Integration Commission is the highest institution co-ordinating the EU integration process in the Lithuanian administration. Its monthly meetings are chaired by the Prime Minister. The Commission is a ministerial level institution undertaking strategic management of integration and accession processes and deciding on key matters related to Lithuania's integration into the EU.

The European integration activities of ministries and other agencies are co-ordinated by the European Committee under the Government of Lithuania. The European Committee is also responsible for the co-ordination of Lithuania's internal preparations for EU accession and implementation of national EU integration programmes. It serves as the secretariat of the European Integration Commission and supervises the implementation of its decisions. The Ministry of Foreign Affairs retains overall responsibility for the European integration process, including the co-ordination of technical assistance.

The main task of the European Law Department is to give its opinion on whether draft laws comply fully with EU law. Without the approval of this department, no draft law or Government regulation can be considered at a sitting of parliament.

Lithuania concluded all but one of the 29 chapters in the screening exercise, the analytical examination of the *acquis*, during which Lithuanian experts study EU legislation and examine to what extent Lithuanian laws comply with the *acquis*.

Lithuanian EU accession strategy is based on implementation of two strategic documents – Lithuania's EU Accession Programme (LEAP, the National Programme for the Adoption of the *Acquis*) and the Lithuania-EU Accession Partnership. LEAP was drafted by the European Committee and adopted by the Governmental European Integration Commission on 31 May 1999. LEAP is a comprehensive integration planning document for 1999-2002 with priorities outlined, measures, institutional and financial resources foreseen. LEAP's summary emphasises internal market, energy sector, justice and home affairs and institutional development as priority areas for the Lithuanian Government. LEAP will be made a living document through regular updates and financial commitments by the Government through budgetary allocations to back up the Programme's implementation. LEAP is also useful in monitoring Lithuania's progress towards EU accession. The European Commission's document, Accession Partnership, arose from the Commission's reports and evaluations and has been extensively used as a monitoring tool to measure Lithuania's progress. It has been used as a planning instrument for financial assistance from the EU to help Lithuania prepare for EU accession faster.

The necessity to approximate laws to the *acquis* makes law harmonisation another priority in national EU integration policy. Lithuania has gone beyond the internal market measures foreseen in the White Paper, and is currently targetting the whole of the *acquis*. The Government plans to transpose the essential part of the *acquis* to the national legislation by 2003-2004.

On the foreign policy level, Lithuania has been participating in the EU Common Foreign and Security Policy (CFSP). From 1996, it has initiated four formal initiatives for the improvement of political dialogue in the framework of the CFSP. Some of the proposals have already been accepted by the EU and implemented. Also, from the signing of

the Europe Agreement in 1995 to July 1999, Lithuania has aligned itself with more than 800 EU statements, common positions and demarches.

An exchange of information on Lithuania's progress towards EU accession between Lithuania and the EU is maintained through annual reporting. On 1 July 1999, the Government submitted to the European Commission the report *Lithuania's Progress Towards Accession to the European Union, July 1998 – June 1999*. The Government noted that since the last report to the Commission, sustained implementation of the remaining reform agenda continued. Restructuring of the economy was advanced by removal of barriers to market entrance and exit, further reduction of direct state involvement, and further liberalisation of rules governing market transactions. Industry and enterprise restructuring accelerated, fuelled by the pressures from the external shock of the Russian crisis and sluggish EU growth. Lithuania maintained macroeconomic stability and by mid-1999, created the legal framework and the main institutional infrastructure to implement the *acquis* in the Single Market area.

PRESIDENT VALDAS ADAMKUS WITH JAVIER SOLANA, NATO SECRETARY GENERAL, IN BRUSSELS, APRIL, 1998

Progress in adopting the *acquis* at the sectoral level has accelerated in 1999. Since the Commission's 1998 Report, Lithuania has made progress towards fulfilling Copenhagen membership criteria, especially in reforming its economy and transposing the EU *acquis*. The economy's success in coping with external shocks demonstrates that Lithuania is a well functioning market economy and fit to withstand competitive pressure. Administrative capacity also strengthened.

The European Commission will finalise the new Accession Partnership and release the Regular Report on Lithuania's progress in October 1999. This document will be analysed by the European Council, and in the December 1999 Helsinki summit a decision will be taken on whether and when to begin accession negotiations with Lithuania.

NATO

Another strategic objective of Lithuania's foreign policy is integration into NATO. Lithuania's history has proved that it is difficult to ensure national security by individual efforts, therefore it aspires to become a member of the Alliance.

Lithuania applied for NATO membership in January 1994. Its aspirations to join NATO are grounded on a solid foundation: stable democracy, the rule of law,

131

economic growth, good relations with neighbouring countries and a solid commitment to the development of Lithuanian defence structures.

The 1996 Law on the Fundamentals of National Security states that national security is ensured by "the state's integration into the European Union, the Western European Union and NATO, with the aim of full membership of these organisations". The provisions of this law ensure that the defence structures will be developed in compliance with the NATO defence system. It also acts as a solid legal basis for continuity and predictability in foreign policy. Integration into NATO is supported by all major political parties in Lithuania, and the public, which regards NATO membership as the only reliable means of ensuring security.

Lithuania, as a stable country with strong democratic civilian control over its armed forces, contributes to the stability and security of the North Atlantic area. Lithuania has signed treaties regulating relations with all neighbouring countries.

Lithuania and Russia have shown an excellent example of how neighbouring states, in spite of their differences regarding security arrangements, can pursue an agenda of co-operation and contribute to European security.

Various regional undertakings and forms of co-operation involving the other two Baltic states, Poland, the Nordic countries, the Council of Baltic Sea States and the BALTSEA initiative to co-ordinate security and defence-related assistance for the Baltic states, are elements within the larger Euro-Atlantic security and political context.

Contributing to Euro-Atlantic co-operation, Lithuania will make full use of the Euro-Atlantic Partnership Council and the enhanced Partnership for Peace (PfP) Programme. Lithuania participates in those areas of the PfP which correspond to its integration aims. One of the main tasks of participation in the PfP is to achieve a high level of interoperability with NATO forces. After implementation of 33 interoperability objectives under the second cycle of the Lithuania-NATO Planning and Review process, the efficiency of the Lithuanian armed forces and their capacity to participate in joint operations with NATO will increase considerably.

LITHUANIAN PEACEKEEPERS TRAINING IN DENMARK

LITHUANIAN PEACEKEEPING TROOPS SERVING IN BOSNIA AND HERZEGOVINA

THE ARMED FORCES

The development of the armed forces is aimed at creating a reliable national defence force. It is carried out in compliance with the NATO interoperability requirements. An increasing number of Lithuanian officers study at NATO and Western military training institutions. In 1996, 87 officers were trained abroad; in 1997 the figure rose to 161; and in 1998 the total was 184.

Economic growth and the planned increase in ratio of defence expenditure to GDP provide a solid foundation for meeting NATO military requirements by allocating the financial resources necessary to that end. Defence expenditure amounted to 0.8% of GDP in 1997; 1.51% in 1999; and is expected to reach 2% in 2001. This level of defence expenditure is set by law.

Since 1994, Lithuania has been co-operating extensively with NATO in ensuring peace in the former Yugoslavia. Its servicemen took part in UNPROFOR and IFOR missions, and continue their service in the SFOR operation. Lithuania was the only Baltic state to send a platoon to participate in NATO-led exercises in Albania in August 1998. At the beginning of 1999, seven

Lithuanians took part in the OSCE Kosovo verification mission.

The armed forces of Lithuania were established by the Seimas on 19 November 1992, although the National Defence Volunteer Force has existed since 1991. The ground forces have 4,300 servicemen.

The core of the ground forces is the Iron Wolf Motorised Infantry Brigade, composed of six battalions and 3,600 soldiers. The brigade can be deployed anywhere in Lithuania.

The mission of the air force is to control, guard and defend Lithuanian airspace. It supports the ground and naval forces and conducts air reconnaissance and airborne landings. The air force takes part in operational training for peacekeepers by flying them into and out of their areas of assignment.

The air force consists of 850 personnel and is equipped with six L-39 training jet aircraft, 27 transport planes, three transport helicopters and four general purpose helicopters. It has two active airfields and an Airspace Surveillance Centre with five radar sites.

The Lithuanian navy consists of 1,200 personnel and the following units: a flotilla of vessels and patrol cutters; the Sea Surveillance and Communication Command; ship maintenance, logistic support, ammunition storage and the Klaipėda 7th Dragoons Coastal Defence Battalion.

The port of Klaipėda is the primary Lithuanian naval facility. The flotilla is equipped with two frigates, a patrol boat, an auxiliary staff ship and two coast guard cutters. The flotilla participates in international manoeuvres and training exercises. The navies of the three Baltic states cooperate in the traditional "BALTOPS" manoeuvres and train jointly. A joint Baltic Squadron will be assigned to mine clearance duties in the Baltic Sea and to international missions.

The National Defence Volunteer Forces (NDVF) consists of 12,000 personnel, including 1,800 full-time officers, NCOs and soldiers. The NDVF is made up of 200 companies and organised into battalions within ten territorial defence formations. The NDVF also has two aviation squadrons that operate 30 light aircraft.

Each NDVF unit down to battalion level is staffed by regular service personnel. There is also a skeleton cadre of regular personnel who direct training and administration. The remainder of the NDVF are volunteers.

The NDVF cooperates with the rest of the armed forces and with border police units. It also provides assistance in the event of natural disasters.

PROSPECTS FOR NATO MEMBERSHIP

An important event, which reconfirmed the continuity of NATO enlargement, was the Washington Summit held on 24 April 1999. Lithuania welcomes the Washington Summit decisions, which included the explicit recognition of aspirant members, the adoption of the Membership Action Plan (MAP) and the review process of candidate readiness to assume membership obligations. NATO's decisions taken at the Washington Summit give substance to the Alliance's "open door" policy, and reaffirm the willingness of NATO to invite new members.

The Washington Summit recognised and welcomed the "continuing efforts and progress in Estonia, Latvia and Lithuania". Equally importantly, the Alliance decided to review the enlargement process at the next summit meeting, to be held no later than 2002.

In preparing to implement the MAP, Lithuania has already established a Co-Ordination Commission on Integration into NATO, which will allow it to better prepare for membership. Lithuania seeks to be the best-qualified candidate for the second round of enlargement.

RELATIONS WITH NEIGHBOURING STATES

Internal stability and respect for the rights of ethnic minorities enable Lithuania to maintain good relations with all neighbouring countries. Regional co-operation and good neighbourly relations are important guidelines in the country's foreign policy. Practical co-operation, including environmental questions, improving transport and communications, cross-border co-operation, and facilitating human and economic exchanges, has contributed to the promotion of security and stability in the region.

Bilateral relations with Poland have been an excellent example of deepening and expanding co-operation, and a confident partnership that still has much potential. Lithuania and Poland renewed diplomatic relations on 5 September 1991. The Declaration on Friendly Relations and Co-Operation of 13 January 1992, laid the foundation for the development of relations. The Agree-

ment on Friendly Relations and Co-Operation of 26 April 1994 confirmed the aspirations of both nations to develop relations and a broad spectrum of co-operation. Over 100 agreements have since been concluded and an intergovernmental institutional framework has been established. Both countries hold joint regular foreign policy consultations, have established a joint Parliamentary Assembly, Presidential Council and Intergovernmental Council.

Key infrastructure and economic projects are being prepared in co-operation with Poland: the Via Baltica motorway, the connection of the electric power networks, and construction of a European-standard railway.

SEIMAS CHAIRMAN PROF. VYTAUTAS LANDSBERGIS AND POLISH PRESIDENT ALEKSANDER KWAŚNIEWSKI, APRIL 1999, VILNIUS

Intensive co-operation between districts, cities and regions was begun after the establishment of the Intergovernmental Commission on Cross-Border Co-Operation. Growing bilateral relations are becoming a factor of stability and a significant element of European co-operation.

The normalisation of relations with Russia has been completed, having started on 29 July 1991 with the signing of the Agreement on the Foundations of Inter-State Relations. Since then, the agreement has been the legal basis for bilateral co-operation between both nations. Another significant step was the withdrawal of Russian troops, completed on 31 August 1993.

A key event occurred on 25 October 1997, when President Algirdas Brazauskas and President Boris Yeltsin signed the Treaty on the State Border between Lithuania and Russia. The Treaty on the Delimitation of the Continental Shelf in the Baltic Sea was also concluded.

Lithuania's relations with the Kaliningrad district of the Russian Federation are an important element in the bilateral relationship. Lithuania aims to promote bilateral and multilateral co-operation with the Kaliningrad district and implement specific programmes concerning the environment and the economy. It seeks to promote cultural and youth exchanges, as well as programmes that increase administrative capacity. During the Russian financial crisis of 1998, Lithuania provided humanitarian assistance to the Kaliningrad district.

Lithuania has maintained good relations with Belarus. A pragmatic dialogue has led to considerable results: the Agreement on Good Neighbourliness and Co-Operation has been concluded; the border has been delimited, and its demarcation is nearing completion.

Regarding the current situation in Belarus, Lithuania encourages its neighbour to solve its domestic problems in line with commonly accepted principles of democracy and the rule of law, while respecting fundamental human rights and freedoms. Lithuania pursues a policy of avoiding the isolation of Belarus, which might have unpredictable consequences for the development of the country as well as for its relations with neighbouring states.

Lithuania is aware that co-operation among the Baltic Sea countries presents a unique opportunity for economic and cultural co-operation. In this context, political and economic partnerships with Latvia and Estonia constitute an important part of Lithuania's regional policy. The existing structures of inter-Baltic co-operation allow Lithuania to focus on practical issues of trade, investment, customs procedures and the development of the transport infrastructure.

Lithuania has actively participated in the Council of the Baltic Sea States, a forum in the Baltic Sea region addressing economic, environmental, social and other practical issues of a regional dimension.

An international conference, Coexistence of Nations and Good Neighbourly Relations – the Guarantee of Security and Stability in Europe - was held in Vilnius in September 1997. Issues of common interest were discussed by the presidents of 11 countries. The prevailing mutual understanding was described as the "spirit of Vilnius" by former German foreign minister Hans Dietrich Genscher. It has now become a tradition to host multilateral forums in Vilnius to strengthen good neighbourly relations and regional co-operation.

LITHUANIA IN INTERNATIONAL ORGANISATIONS

Lithuania accords high priority in its foreign policy to multilateral co-operation and implementations of the United Nations' goals of the maintainenance of peace and security and the betterment of humanity. Lithuania became a member of the United Nations on 17 September 1991, and ever since it has participated actively in various UN undertakings.

FOREIGN MINISTER ALGIRDAS SAUDARGAS AND UN SECRETARY GENERAL KOFI ANNAN, SEPTEMBER, 1997, NEW YORK

Since 1994, Lithuania has been a full-fledged troop-contributing country to UN peacekeeping operations in Croatia (UNPROFOR), Eastern Slavonia (UNTAES and UN police support group), Bosnia and Herzegovina and lately Kosovo. Since the deployment of the first Lithuanian platoon within the Danish Peacekeeping Battalion, a total of 19 civilian policemen and as many as 100 troops have served the cause of peace within the UN missions. Moreover, Lithuanian military platoons have served in the NATO-led IFOR and SFOR missions in Bosnia and Herzegovina. Lithuanian military forces are to join KFOR. Two peacekeeping battalions, LITPOLBAT and BALTBAT, established together with Poland, Latvia and Estonia, are fully operational and in the process of further development. In 1996, a mine explosion caused the first casualty to the Lithuanian "blue helmets".

In January 1998, Lithuania joined the Standby Arrangement System for United Nations peacekeeping operations. It was one of the first countries to sign the UN Memorandum of Understanding, by which 24 Lithuanian civilian police officers, military observers and staff officers remain on standby and can be quickly deployment to a new mission at the request of the UN.

Lithuania is a member-state of all major non-proliferation, disarmament and arms control treaties.

The Government has established effective procedures for export control of strategic goods and technologies. Having signed in 1998 the Model additional protocol with the International Atomic Energy Agency for the Application of Safeguards, Lithuania contributes to a strengthened safeguards system.

It fully supports efforts aimed at securing universal acceptance of and compliance with the standards set out in the UN human rights treaties and by the Council of Europe. The Seimas has ratified the 1966 International Convention on the Elimination of All Forms of Racial Discrimination, thereby completing the accession process to all major universal human rights instruments. Lithuania has also joined the world donor community by contributing to the International Red Cross Committee and the Voluntary Fund for Technical Co-operation of the High Commissioner for Human Rights.

Lithuania is a member of all UN Specialised Agencies. Its experience and position are made available at every major global conference held under the auspices of the UN.

ECONOMY

INTRODUCTION

Following the restoration of independence, Lithuania embarked on a massive transformation of its largely state-run economy along free market principles. The initial period entailed many painful choices, as price liberalisation triggered inflation exceeding 1,000% and budget discipline re-

DVARČIONIŲ KERAMIKA, CERAMIC TILE PRODUCTION

sulted in the shedding of tens of thousands of redundant industrial jobs (since the Government stopped the traditional practice of massively bailing out inefficient enterprises).

In a short year and a half (1991-92), the Government launched a nationwide privatisation drive, which laid the foundations for the rapid growth of the small and medium-sized enterprise sector (there are over 100,000 registered private enterprises) and private agriculture. Within this short period, housing and the retail sector reverted to mainly private ownership.

Foreign trade began a painful reorientation from almost total dependence on the Russian and CIS markets to a more balanced relationship between East and West (today the EU is Lithuania's largest trading partner).

Despite a change of Government in late 1992, Lithuania persevered in continuing stringent stabilisation policies, which the people accepted as necessary, and price stability was achieved. At the same time output began recovering. The recovery gained momentum from 1996 to the summer of 1998, recording impressive annual growth rates of 7.3% in 1997 and 5.1% in 1998. Although the Russian financial crisis hurt some Lithuanian firms which exported heavily to the CIS, the damage nevertheless was contained, and growth has continued. Lithuania's financial sector remained intact, the litas remained stable, and inflation continued declining to rates considered normal for Western European countries.

Lithuania has the largest and most diversified economy among the Baltic states. During the last 50 years massive industrialisation gave birth to enterprises specialising in electronics, chemicals, machine tools, metal processing, wood products, construction materials and food processing. The light industry sector includes the production of textiles, ready-to-wear clothing, furniture and household appliances.

Keyed to industrialisation was the development of a relatively modern infrastructure, with four major airports, a large ice-free port and a four-lane, motorway network, which was considered to be the best in the Soviet Union, and is still among the best in the entire region. Large-scale privatisation of the infrastructure and many of the larger formerly state-owned industrial enterprises, which commenced in 1996, will ensure continued investment and modernisation.

GDP AND INFLATION

With the foundation for a healthy market economy in place, GDP growth (3.3%) started in 1995. Privatisation, the success of newly established enterprises, the growth of services and foreign trade as well as other factors ensured sustained expansion. In 1996 GDP increased 4.7%; in 1997 it went up 7.3%; and in 1998 Lithuania had one of the fastest growing economies in the region. In the first six months of 1998, GDP grew by 7.3%, but the economic crisis in Russia slowed this impressive rate to 5.1% for the year as a whole.

GDP growth in 1999 is expected to continue as more and more enterprises diversify their trade links and find markets in the West. The Ministry of the Economy estimates that the country's average annual GDP expansion will be between 4.1% and 5.7% from 1999 to the year 2000.

The private sector has been absorbing steadily increasing shares of GDP from 1990 to the present (70% in 1998). As large-

SECTORAL DISTRIBUTION OF GDP

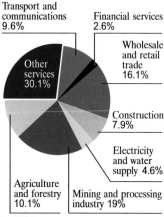

Transport and communications 9.6%

Financial services 2.6%

Wholesale and retail trade 16.1%

Other services 30.1%

Construction 7.9%

Electricity and water supply 4.6%

Agriculture and forestry 10.1%

Mining and processing industry 19%

* 1998 figures

Source: Lithuanian Department of Statistics

YEARLY INFLATION RATE

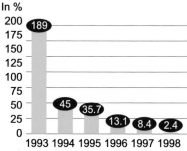

In %

200 — 189
175
150
125
100
75
50 — 45 35.7
25 — 13.1 8.4 2.4
0
1993 1994 1995 1996 1997 1998

Source: Lithuanian Department of Statistics

143

scale privatisation continues in 1999, this total should be even greater by 2000. GDP per capita has been rising rapidly from 1990 to 1999, reflecting increasing modernisation and rationalisation processes at the workplace. In 1999 this figure should be USD 3,250, and it is estimated that in 2001 GDP per capita will total USD 4,500.

Industry accounts for about a 25% share of GDP, while the services sector has been expanding steadily and now amounts to 30.8% of the total. Agriculture generates 11% of GDP, but its relative share is declining.

For several years now the inflation rate in Lithuania has consistently been among the lowest in Central and Eastern Europe, declining to 2.4% per annum in 1998.

MONEY AND BANKING

Reform of Lithuania's state-owned banking sector started as early as 1988, with the introduction of a standard two-tier banking system consisting of the central bank and commercial banks. At present the Bank of Lithuania has the exclusive right to grant and revoke licences to local and foreign banks and to supervise their activities.

Private commercial banking boomed from 1992 to 1994, while regulatory agencies, still in their infancy, could not keep up. In late 1995 a banking crisis was triggered by the suspension of two commercial banks by the central bank. This short-lived crisis weeded out a number of problem banks and focused the authorities' attention on the need for more effective regulation. Far

BANKS			
Bank	Assets	Share Capital	Loans
Lietuvos taupomasis bankas (Lithuanian Savings Bank)	795.2	41.8	269.1
Vilniaus bankas	649.9	37.5	293.1
Lietuvos žemės ūkio bankas (Lithuanian Agricultural Bank)	347.9	47.3	233.5
Bankas Hermis	382.2	22.5	216.2
Bankas Snoras	116.0	12.2	33.2
Ūkio bankas (Economy Bank)	49.6	15.0	23.7
Šiaulių bankas	35.8	8.5	21.8
Medicinos bankas (Medical Bank)	20.4	6.5	7.2
Industrijos bankas (Industry Bank)	16.5	16.5	5.5
Total	2413.5	207.8	1103.3
Source: The Bank of Lithuania, 1998 (all figures in million USD)			

144

more rigorous sanctions for non-compliance of regulations limiting the risk of commercial banking were introduced. International Auditing Standards became mandatory and a system of deposit insurance was implemented.

By mid-1996 the banking sector was growing again. The share capital of banks increased 18% in 1997. The following year, the share capital surged 37% and is continuing robust growth. Foreign capital, attracted by the strong growth prospects of the economy, boosted its share of Lithuanian banking capital from 25% of the total in early 1997 to over 33% at the end of the same year. Recent trends suggest that this total will continue increasing.

At the beginning of 1999, there were two branches of foreign banks and four representative offices of foreign banks. Ten commercial banks were operating in this period, of which only two, the Savings and Agriculture banks were state-owned. Plans call for their privatisation in 1999.

Commercial banks have dramatically expanded their range of services, including leasing, insurance, asset management and investment banking. Credit cards have become increasingly popular in Lithuania.

THE STOCK EXCHANGE

Private securities in Lithuania are traded on the National Stock Exchange (NSEL), which opened in 1993. This was the first stock exchange in the Baltic states to be opened in the post-Soviet period. It was developed with the assistance of the French government and the Paris Bourse.

The Securities Commission and the NSEL are regulated by the Law on Public Trading and Securities, adopted in 1996. Control over the Lithuanian securities market is exercised by the Securities Commission, established in 1992, which registers all securities issued in Lithuania.

The total market capitalisation of the NSEL amounted to 13.5 billion litas (USD 3.37 billion) in 1998, which was twice that of the Riga and Tallinn exchanges combined. Investment by non-residents is not restricted. Local brokerage firms provide a full range of services.

THE LITAS

The litas was the legal tender of pre-war Lithuania. It was introduced in 1922 and circulated until the occupation in 1940. In 1993, Lithuania reintroduced the litas (at the official exchange rate of four litas to one USD) within the context of a strict monetary regime. In 1994 a currency board system was established, under which the amount of litas in circulation was pegged to the amount of gold and foreign currency reserves held by the Bank of Lithuania. The litas-USD exchange rate has remained unchanged since its reintroduction in 1993, making it one of the most stable currencies of all the countries of Central and Eastern Europe.

Having achieved monetary stability, the current Government is nevertheless committed to a gradual withdrawal from the Currency Board system, leading to a transitional peg to a euro/USD combination in the future. Lithuania is implementing the requirements that European economic and monetary union imposes on candidate countries, and preparing for membership in the EU and integration into the European central banking system.

THE 200-LITAS NOTE, DEPICTING THE LITHUANIAN PHILOSOPHER VYDŪNAS

INDUSTRY

Today's diversified industrial sector developed from workshops set up a century ago to exploit local timber and agricultural resources. Soviet industrial development essentially concentrated on manufacturing high value added production, relying on the technical skills of Lithuanian workers. The growth of foreign investment, particularly over the past three years, has been accompanied by significant modernisation of the following sectors: chemicals, wood processing, shipbuilding, electronics, telecommunications, textiles, dairy products and beer brewing.

Traditionally, the mainstay of the Lithuanian economy has been food production. Before the Second World War, Lithuania exported meat and dairy products first mainly to Germany and then to Great Britain in the 1930s. Agricultural overproduction was a constant problem.

During Soviet times Lithuania and the other two Baltic states supplied an important share of the food products consumed by the northwest part of the Soviet Union, including the city of Leningrad.

Today, producers of milk, cheese and beverages have succeeded in considerably upgrading

146

production thanks to major foreign investment. In 1999 some 14 Lithuanian milk processors received EU certificates of quality which allow them to export to the EU.

Another major industrial sector which was inherited from the previous era is the oil refining and distribution industry, which accounts for 29% of the output of all Lithuanian industries. *Mažeikių nafta* is one of the largest oil refineries in Eastern Europe, with an annual refining capacity of 12 million tonnes. The refinery has been receiving all of its crude oil from Russia, but it will soon have the option to import oil via the recently completed Būtingė oil terminal on the Baltic coast.

Other significant sectors of Lithuanian industry are textiles and wearing apparel (with an 11% market share), chemicals (8%), machinery, radio, TV and communications equipment (8.3%), and timber products (2.2%). Lithuania's enterprises produce refrigerators, TV tubes, automotive electrical components, bicycles and chemical fertilisers.

Production output of Lithuanian industry exceeded 23 billion litas (USD 5.75 billion) in 1998. About 52% of industrial production is sold in foreign markets.

TOP 10 LITHUANIAN ENTERPRISES

NAME	ACTIVITY	TURNOVER (IN USD)	NUMBER OF EMPLOYEES
MAŽEIKIŲ NAFTA	OIL REFINING	606,941,457	3,685
LIETUVOS ENERGIJA	PRODUCTION OF ELECTRIC POWER AND ITS DISTRIBUTION	513,100,000	11,480
LIETUVOS GELEŽINKELIAI	RAIL TRANSPORT	177,466,650	16,962
LIETUVOS DUJOS	TRADE AND DISTRIBUTION OF NATURAL GAS	168,758,106	4,265
LIETUVOS TELEKOMAS	COMMUNICATIONS	165,710,548	9,896
IGNALINA NUCLEAR PLANT	PRODUCTION OF ELECTRIC POWER	157,236,481	5,078
LUKOIL-BALTIJA	RETAIL TRADE IN PETROL	123,000,128	65
ACHEMA	CHEMICAL PRODUCTION	111,732,000	2,158
EKRANAS	PRODUCTION OF TV TUBES	77,474,750	5,646
KLAIPĖDA STEVEDORING COMPANY	CARGO TRANSPORT	45,485,886	2,370

PRODUCTION OF ELECTRICITY METERS, EMH-ELGAMA, VILNIUS

AGRICULTURE AND FORESTRY

A total of 51% of the land area of Lithuania is cultivated. Over 353,000 people, or 21.5% of the country's workforce, is employed in agriculture, hunting and forestry.

Until 1990, the great bulk of the land belonged to state-run collective farms, although small plots of land were parcelled out for private use. Private farming can be said to have begun in 1989, with the passage of legislation providing for the establishment of privately-managed (but not yet owned farms). By 1990 several thousand farmers had begun private farming. Agricultural reform was aimed at the creation of a strong and competitive agricultural sector, based on private farming. The Government proceeded with a massive restitution campaign in 1991, which ensured the eventual return of property rights to former owners or their successors.

In 1998 there were 201,000 private household farms. In addition, almost 327,600 rural households cultivated small land holdings (two to three hectares) mostly for personal consumption. The average size of a farm is only 11.8 hectares, although some consolidation of farm holdings, either through purchase or leasing of land, has taken place.

In 1998, the grain harvest amounted to 3,254,000 tonnes, while milk production was 1,924,000 tonnes. A total of 291,000 tonnes of meat was produced. Over the past several years there has been a discernible tendency to increase the land area devoted to cereal production at the expense of grazing.

Forests are one of Lithuania's chief natural resources, covering almost two million hectares, or 30.3% of the country (which translates into a half-hectare of forest per inhabitant). Approximately 60% of the forests are coniferous, mainly pine and fir.

PRIVATISATION OF THE FOOD PROCESSING SECTOR HAS GIVEN CONSUMERS A GREAT VARIETY OF NEW AND TRADITIONAL FOOD PRODUCTS

About three to four million cubic metres of timber are produced annually. Timber and timber products make up 5% of the country's exports. More than 53% of the forests belongs to the state. Forest land is subdivided into 43 forest districts and five national parks. It is estimated that in the future private forests will amount to an increasing share of the total land area of forests.

ENERGY

In 1998, Lithuania used 9.89 Mtne (million tonnes of oil) of energy resources, of which oil products constituted 38%, natural gas 18%, nuclear power 36%, and other resources (hydroenergy, coal, peat, wood) 8%. Most of the energy resources were used for producing electricity (42%) and heating (19%).

Lithuania's main source of electric power is the Ignalina Nuclear Power Plant, with its 3,000 MW capacity. In 1998 it generated 13,554 million kWh of electric power, or 80% of the country's total electricity supply. This is one of the highest rates of reliance on nuclear power for electricity in the world. The Government has applied every effort to ensure that the plant comply with international nuclear safety standards. The Swedish government, the European Bank for Reconstruction and Development, the USA, Norway and Japan have provided a total of over USD 220 million in assistance to upgrade safety standards at the plant. A second phase of safety enhancement is expected to involve an additional USD 100 million, most of which will come from Lithuanian funds.

In addition, Lithuania operates 13 thermal electricity plants, the Kruonis Hydro-Accumulative Power Plant, the Kaunas Hydroelectric Plant and 17 small power plants. The output of the largest thermal electricity plant is 1,800 MW; and the present capacity of the Kruonis Hydro-Accumulative Power Plant is 800 MW, although there are plans to increase its generating power. The latter installation includes an enormous artificial basin constructed on a rise overlooking the reservoir of the Kaunas Hydroelectric Plant. During nonpeak hours, water from the reservoir is pumped into the artificial basin (measuring some 4km in circumference) to be released in periods of high electricity demand. The Kruonis facility is expected to play an important future role when Lithuania begins exports of electricity to the West.

A large amount of electric power is exported (mainly to the East) because local demand is considerably smaller than the built-in capacity.

PRIVATISATION

Lithuania's privatisation programme has been at the core of the country's economic reforms and is considered a crucial part of the transformation to the free-market economy.

The first stage of privatisation for vouchers took place between 1991 and 1995. During that period, 5,714 state enterprises (30% of the total state property), 93.5% of housing, and most agricultural assets were privatised. In terms of the rate of privatisation, Lithuania followed closely behind the acknowledged regional leaders in this process: the Czech Republic, Hungary and Estonia.

That stage of privatisation fundamentally changed the outlook of the whole population, creating a country of property owners and entrepreneurs, and enabling Lithuania to maintain and develop a strong local top management capacity.

The second stage of privatisation started in August 1996 and involved sales of assets for cash to both local and foreign investors. This ongoing phase of privatisation is taking place through open transactions, including public subscription for shares, auctions of enterprises and other assets, and offerings of shares through public tenders. International tenders have been held for larger enterprises.

In total, over 600 entities (including a variety of assets ranging from hotels to factories) were sold in the second wave of privatisation.

On 7 July 1998, the largest ever privatisation contract in the Baltic states was signed, resulting in the purchase of 60% of Lithuanian Telecom by Amber Teleholding, a consortium of the Swedish Telia and Finnish Sonera firms for USD 510 million and a further USD 221 million in investment within two years.

In 1998 the State Property Fund was established. It represents the Government in privatising enterprises and other property, and manages state-owned shares. This institution takes over the obligations of enterprises, negotiates with foreign investors, and maintains a privatisation data base.

In 1998, a list of additional entities slated for privatisation was approved, consisting of 2,245 entities in which remaining state-owned shares constitute 3.4 billion litas (USD 850 million). Among these entities are large enterprises such as *Lietuvos kuras* (Lithuanian Fuel Company) and the Lithuanian Shipping Company (LISCO). The privatisation of two state-controlled commercial banks, *Lietuvos taupomasis bankas* (Lithuanian Savings Bank) and *Lietuvos žemės ūkio bankas* (Lithuanian Agricultural Bank), is also under way.

Private Enterprise

The Lithuanian economy is now based on private enterprise and ownership and a free-market system. In recent years, Lithuanian society has reoriented itself to this system, from which it was uprooted 50 years ago, when practically the country's entire private property was nationalised or expropriated by the Soviets.

Between 1991 and 1997 the contribution of the private sector to GDP grew more than four times, and reached 70%. The private sector also employs about 70% of the workforce.

As a result of privatisation and economic restructuring, a large number of small enterprises appeared in industry, trade, and other sectors. On 1 January 1999, there was a total of 145,508 enterprises registered in Lithuania. The majority are private enterprises (93,434) and limited companies (38,697).

The development of small and medium-sized enterprises (SMEs) is regulated by the Law on the Development of Small and Medium-Sized Enterprises, passed in 1998 and supported by the Fund for Support of Small and Medium-Sized Businesses.

A model for creating regional SME development programmes has been prepared. There are six business advisory centres, as well as the Agency for the Development of Small and Medium-Sized Businesses.

STRONG DEMAND FOR ENERGY- EFFICIENT DOORS AND WINDOWS HAS GIVEN RISE TO MANY NEW SPECIALISED FIRMS

FOREIGN TRADE

Lithuania pursues a liberal foreign trade policy, and this has stimulated rapid foreign trade growth: from 1994 to 1998 Lithuanian exports rose by 91.2% and imports grew by 136.3%. The balance of trade remains negative, however. It is estimated at USD 2.08 billion for 1998.

In 1999 Germany became the main trading partner, followed by Latvia and Belarus. Although Russia was Lithuania's largest trading partner until recently, it has now dropped to fourth place because of the 1998 Russian financial crisis.

The increasing trade volume with the European Union was predicated on the free trade agree-

Foreign trade by major partners (in %) 1998		
Exports	By Region	Imports
37.4	EU	47.3
2.2	EFTA	2.0
35.7	CIS	26.2
	By Country	
16.7	Russia	21.1
12.9	Germany	18.1
8.8	Belarus	2.2
8.0	Ukraine	1.9
11.2	Latvia	1.8
4.0	Denmark	3.8
3.4	The United Kingdom	3.7
4.0	Italy	4.5
2.8	The Netherlands	2.3
2.5	Estonia	1.5
2.3	Poland	3.4
13.4	Other countries	23.5

Source: Lithuanian Department of Statistics

ment between Lithuania and the European Union, which came into force in 1995. With the exception of textiles and some agricultural products, exported Lithuanian good were exempted from duty. Imports from the EU rose by 47.3% (USD 1.38 billion) and exports from Lithuania to the EU increased by 37.4% (USD 2.73 billion).

Textiles, clothing, fertilisers, equipment and machinery are Lithuania's main exported commodities. In 1998 Lithuania exported goods worth 14.8 billion litas, including textiles and textile products worth 2.78 billion litas; fertilisers and other chemical substances for 1.4 billion litas; petrol and other mineral products for 2.8 billion litas; machinery and equipment for 1.7 billion litas; and foodstuffs for 560 million litas. Imported commodities include crude oil, natural gas, cars and machinery.

Lithuania has also signed free-trade agreements with the European Free Trade Association, Latvia, Estonia, the Czech Republic, Slovakia, Poland, Slovenia, Ukraine and Turkey. Most favoured status is applied in trade with 22 foreign countries. Lithuania is negotiating for membership of the World Trade Organisation.

INVESTMENT

After an initially slow start, Lithuania has developed into an attractive location for foreign investors. The main reasons are its skilled, low-cost labour (which can be a realistic alternative to production in the West) along with its favourable geographic position next to the huge markets of the East and the Baltic rim, comprising some 300 million consumers.

In 1996 alone, more than 60% of new FDI came from existing investors, who decided to expand their operations in the country. By the end of 1997, cumulative FDI totalled over USD 1 billion. After the privatisation of the Lithuanian Telecom in 1998, cumulative FDI jumped USD 510 million, approaching USD 2 billion. As the banking system and banking capacity grow stronger, an increasing amount of credit will be made available for financing investment. It is estimated that from 1999 to 2000 over three billion litas in investment will come from the national banks.

There are 6,583 registered foreign companies or joint ventures linking Lithuanian economic entities with foreign capital. The founding capital of these enterprises amounts to 6.74 billion litas, of which 3.44 billion litas, or 51% of the total amount, is of foreign origin.

TRANSPORT DEVELOPMENT STRATEGY

Lithuania's geographical situation is highly favourable for the

FOREIGN INVESTMENT GROWTH

USD MLN

19 — 1992
149 — 1993
310 — 1994
352 — 1995
700 — 1996
1,041 — 1997
1,975 — 1998
2,500* — 1999

*Prognosis

Source: Lithuanian Development Agency

development of the transport sector. In 1994 the Government approved the National Programme for Transport Development to the Year 2010. The programme formulated the main aims of national transport policy, drew up plans for the development of specific areas of transport, and provided for measures to facilitate Lithuania's integration into the European transport network and the transport services market. The Government rated transport as a priority area of the economy.

SEA TRANSPORT

The Lithuanian sea transport system has been integrating itself into the international shipping and seaport services market, thus ensuring stable profits and preserving employment.

The 1996 Law on the Klaipėda State Seaport determined the broad framework of privatisation of the port's assets. It stipulated that the port's waters, land and infrastructure shall remain state property; while all other entities, including some profitable shipping and ship building and repair enterprises, can be privatised.

Klaipėda is a key junction in Branch 9B (linking east-west roads and sea routes) of the Ninth International Multi-Modal European Priority Transport Corridor, also known as a Crete Corridor. It is the northernmost ice-free port on the eastern Baltic coast, linking Lithuania via regular shipping lines with many Western European, American, Asian and African ports, as well as by ferry lines with German, Swedish and Danish ports and the railway network and roads in the Baltic and Eastern European countries. The total area of the port of Klaipėda is 1,038 hectares, including its land area (415ha) and waters (623ha). The port also maintains about 136 hectares of reserve territory. The total amount of covered warehouses is 74,900 square metres, and the area of open warehouses is about 260,000 square metres. Ocean-going ships can dock alongside wharfs extending 19 kilometres in length.

There are seven specialised stevedoring companies operating in the port. Of these the Klaipėda Stevedoring Company (KLASCO) is the largest, handling more than half of the port's total turnover. A large container line, the Curonian Line, links Klaipėda with the largest Western European cargo terminals at Felixstowe and Rotterdam. KLASCO also owns an international ferry line, which receives passenger ferries and other ro-

ro vessels transporting lorries, trailers, autotrailers, cars and other cargo. It was recently privatised.

The Lithuanian-US company *Klaipėdos nafta* (Klaipėda Oil) completed renovation work in 1998, thus becoming one of the most modern oil products terminals in Europe. The amount of cargo handled by this enterprise last year amounted to 20% to 25% of the port's total turnover. Its capacity is 7.1 million tonnes of cargo per year.

In Klaipėda there is also the Baltija Shipyard, and three other ship repair enterprises. The Baltija Shipyard is owned by the Odense Lindo Shipyard, which belongs to Maersk, the Danish industrial and financial group. The shipyard builds superstructures of large container vessels and has completed a fleet of modern tugboats. It has also started the construction of a fleet of vessels designed to serve oil rigs at sea.

The public company Western Ship Repair, also recently privatised by Norwegian capital, repairs large sea vessels and has three floating docks with a lifting capacity of 8,500, 12,000 and 27,000 tonnes. The company repairs ocean-going ships and ferries belonging to Western European shipping companies.

Klaipėda's new container terminal

TRANSIT TRAFFIC BY RAIL, 1998 (IN MLN TNS)

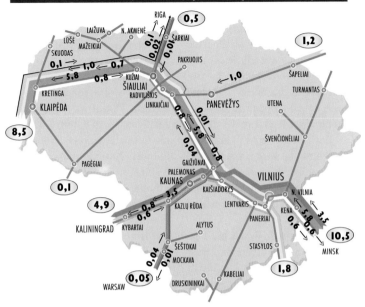

Laivitė, a public company, repairs medium-sized ships and has a floating dock with a lifting capacity of 6,000 tonnes. *Klaipėdos laivų remontas* (Klaipėda Ship Repair) repairs and renovates medium-sized and small vessels.

Along with these companies, the port of Klaipėda also maintains two hydrotechnical enterprises, numerous small ship repair companies and agencies, shipping agents, and freight forwarders. The Lithuanian Association of Shipping Brokers and Agents, and the Klaipėda Association of Shipping Agents and Freight Forwarders are also based there.

From 450 to 550 ships weigh anchor at Klaipėda each month. Passenger ferries are also handled by the port. In 1997 over 70,000 passengers passed through the port, mainly on the Klaipėda-Kiel and Klaipėda-Mukran routes.

RAILWAYS

Railways are one of the most important means of transport in Lithuania for long-distance freight transport. The rail system has good connections with the rail networks of the Baltic states and CIS countries. The main route between Russia and the Kaliningrad district passes via Lithuania.

157

The total length of the railways is 1,997 kilometres (the density is 30.6km per 1,000 sq km). Among the most commonly transported commodities are crude oil and refined oil products, peat, metals, agricultural machinery, cars and other vehicles, chemical and mineral fertilisers, and coal.

In 1993 a direct rail link with the Polish rail system was opened after the extension of a European standard-gauge railway line from the Polish border to the town of Šeštokai.

Lithuanian railways are also used by Latvian, Estonian, Russian, Belarusian and Ukrainian passenger transit trains, or separate carriages belonging to these states. Lithuania is linked by direct rail routes with Russia, Belarus, Latvia, Poland and Germany.

CIVIL AVIATION

Lithuanian civil aviation has long and rich traditions, starting from the first years of pre-war independence. During the post-war era, Lithuania served as one of the main centres for the repair of aircraft. That is why although a relatively small country, it now has four international airports: in Vilnius, Kaunas, Palanga and Šiauliai, in addition to 20 aerodromes. Over the last five years foreign loans have been earmarked for the modernisation of flight management and aeronavigation equipment and the upgrading of Vilnius Airport. Now the airport is fully compatible with ICAO standards for international airports. Vilnius, Kaunas and Palanga airports together handle over 500,000 passengers annually. A total of 88%

ONE OF LITHUANIAN AIRLINES' NEW SAAB AIRCRAFT

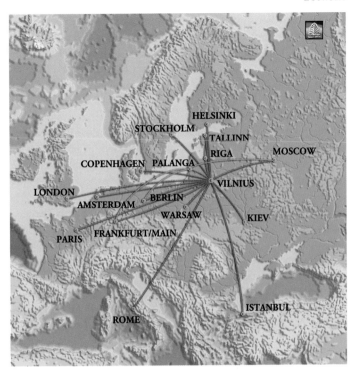

HELSINKI
STOCKHOLM
TALLINN
RIGA
MOSCOW
COPENHAGEN PALANGA
VILNIUS
LONDON
AMSTERDAM BERLIN
WARSAW
KIEV
PARIS FRANKFURT/MAIN
ISTANBUL
ROME

of this number is served by Vilnius Airport. This facility has the capacity to handle over 100 aircraft per day, and 600 passengers an hour. Passenger volume has been generally growing at an average rate of 11% to 12% per annum.

Vilnius has become an attractive destination for European air carriers, including Finnair, British Airways, Lufthansa, LOT, Estonian Air, SAS and Aeroflot.

Two Lithuanian airlines, the national carrier Lithuanian Airlines (LAL) and its affiliate Air

LITHUANIAN AIRLINES REGULAR FLIGHTS

Lithuania, carry up to 300,000 passengers annually to 20 destinations in Europe and Asia. Lithuanian Airlines has made great strides in modernising its air fleet, and now relies on Western-made aircraft for its scheduled flights. The workhorse of the LAL fleet is the Boeing 737 aircraft, of which there is one of the 737-500 series, one 737-300 and

159

two 737-200s. For shorter flights LAL employs two SAAB 2000 and two SAAB 340B aircraft.

ROAD TRANSPORT

Lithuania has 21,100 kilometres of paved roads, including 10,850 kilometres with an improved surface. Every 1,000 square kilometres of the country has 323 kilometres of paved roads and 166 kilometres with improved surface. The ratios per 1,000 inhabitants are 5.6 and 2.8 kilometres, respectively.

Lithuania maintains a well-developed road network. In 1996 four main roads were accepted as European-standard roads (E67, E271, E272, E85). Four-lane motorways linking Vilnius with Klaipėda (300km) and Panevėžys with Vilnius (150km) provide motorists with fast and safe road connections to four major cities.

In 1994 road freight transport was fully privatised. Only public bus companies remain unprivatised; they are mainly owned by municipalities. The Road Transport Inspectorate has granted over 5,000 licences to road transport businesses over the last four years.

Since 1994 the average traffic density on Lithuanian roads has increased by 15-20% per year. The growth in transit transport in recent years confirms the good prospects for growth in transit services. Lithuanian freight operators have increased their international volume almost 16-fold from 1993 to 1999. In 1996 Lithuanian carriers completed 239,000 individual haulage contracts abroad; in 1998 this total stood at over 400,000.

Private car registrations have been growing at a rate of 10-15% each year, despite hefty increases in the excise tax on petrol. High-grade petrol now costs the equivalent of USD 0.55 per litre. Approximately one million private cars are in use throughout Lithuania, which puts an increasing strain on the road network. Renovation and development of the road network intensified after the Law on the Road Fund entered into force in 1996.

Lithuania joined the Trans-European North-South Motorway (TEN) Co-operation Trust Fund Agreement. The country has adopted European markings for its international roads.

The Via Baltica motorway, linking Helsinki with Warsaw via the Baltic states, is being constructed with loans from the European Investment Bank, the European Bank for Reconstruction and Development, and the Nordic Investment Bank.

LITHUANIA'S MAIN ROADS ARE COMPARABLE TO WESTERN HIGHWAYS

Gas and Oil Pipeline Network

The supply network consists of a gas main with branches, and one oil pipeline. Natural gas is imported from Russia through a 1,400-kilometre main pipeline, and distributed through 3,900 kilometres of branch pipes.

The Polock-Biržai-Mažeikiai pipeline, which has been in operation since 1978, transports crude oil purchased in Russia. Part of the crude is channeled to Mažeikiai for refining and the rest is sent to the Latvian port of Ventspils for transshipment. The annual capacity of this pipeline is 16 million tonnes.

In mid-1999, the newly-constructed Būtingė offshore oil terminal began operations. Its projected annual capacity is eight million tonnes of crude oil.

Communications

This is perhaps the fastest growing sector of the Lithuanian economy. It has been attracting an increasing amount of public and private investment, which has translated into new technology and overall modernisation. Major changes in the ownership and

Following extensive investment, Klaipėda now has a modern oil terminal

management structures of telecommunications companies have occurred recently.

The public company Lithuanian Telecom has almost 1,100,000 fixed telephone subscriber lines. Subscribers are now able to take advantage of the new opportunities that modern technology offers: for example, farmers are increasingly using cordless connections and radio telephones. Also, fibre-optic cables are increasingly being utilised: they will connect the existing and future digital telephone stations into the Lithuanian circular digital network of telecommunications.

Communications networks are being upgraded by joint Lithuanian and foreign mobile communications companies: *Bitė GSM, Omnitel,* and *Comliet.* The mobile communications market has grown more than 11-fold in just two years. At the beginning of 1996 there were only 15,000 mobile phone users in the country. By January 1999 this figure had grown to almost 300,000. Operating licenses have been granted to six mobile communications, four paging, eight data transmission and satellite communications and 50 regional cable television operators.

The postal service, celebrating its 80th anniversary in 1998, has established the EMS, an express mail and package delivery service. It competes with a number of private carriers, including several international companies.

The Lithuanian Radio and Television Centre uses 57 television and 76 radio transmitters. Radio and television programmes are broadcast by 29 radio-relay stations and a 1,231-kilometre radio relay line. There are two medium wave radio networks and three ultra-short FM ones.

The Government has adopted the National Programme for the Development of Communications and Informatics to the Year 2005. The Law on Telecommunications stipulates that, from 31 December 2002, Lithuanian Telecom will lose its exclusive rights, and the telecommunications market will be fully liberalised. Plans call for switching all telephone subscribers to a digital network by 2015. It is estimated that in the year 2000 the penetration of fixed telephone subscriber lines per 100 inhabitants will be 37. Radio and television will switch to European frequencies and standards. The development of the television network will provide the opportunity to broadcast 20 to 30 radio and television programmes, send teletext messages, offer paging and other services.

TOP INVESTORS IN LITHUANIA (AS OF 1 SEPTEMBER 1999)

INVESTOR	ORIGIN	ACTIVITIES	USD (MLN.)
AMBER TELEHOLDINGS AS (TELIA/SONERA)	SWEDEN/FINLAND	TELECOMMUNICATIONS	510.00
TELIA/SONERA	SWEDEN/FINLAND	TELECOMMUNICATIONS	66.30
PHILIP MORRIS INTERNATIONAL FINANCE CORPORATION	USA	TOBACCO PRODUCTS	60.00
SKANDINAVISKA ENSKILDA BANKEN AB	SWEDEN	BANKING	57.00
TELE DENMARK A/S MILLICOM EAST HODING B. V.	DENMARK/LUXEMBOURG	TELECOMMUNICATIONS	49.25
CARLSBERG	DENMARK	BREWERY	45.00
DEN NORSKE STATS OLJESE	NORWAY	PETROLEUM PRODUCTS	37.93
DANISCO SUGAR A/S	DENMARK	SUGAR PRODUCTION	34.00
THE COCA-COLA COMPANY	USA	SOFT DRINKS	31.50
SHELL OVERSEAS HOLDINGS LIMITED	GREAT BRITAIN/NETHERLANDS	PETROLEUM PRODUCTS	28.85
CODAN INSURANCE LTD. A/S	DENMARK	INSURANCE	27.00
AS HANSA LISING	ESTONIA	FINANCIAL SERVICES	25.58
EURO OIL INVEST S. A	LUXEMBOURG	PETROLEUM PRODUCTS	25.37
HENLEY TRADINGG LTD./PRIVATE PERSON	IRELAND/SWITZERLAND	ELECTRONICS	25.14
NESTE OY	FINLAND	PETROLEUM PRODUCTS	25.00
BALTIC BEVERAGES HOLDING (APRIPPS-HARTWALL COMPANY)	SWEDEN/FINLAND	BREWERY	24.00
KRAFT FOOD INTERNATIONAL	USA	CONFECTIONERY	23.50
CALWER DECKEN-UND TUCHFABRIKEN	GERMANY	TEXTILES	22.38
PARTEC INSULATION FINNFUND; NEFCO	SWEDEN/FINLAND	CONSTRUCTION MATERIALS	19.75
ODENSE STEEL SHIPYARD LTD	DENMARK	SHIP BUILDING	18.01
OSMAN TRADING AB	SWEDEN	OIL TERMINAL	16.79
WOODISON TRADING AB	IRELAND		
FERROUS INVESTMENT LTD	GREAT BRITAIN		
DISTRAL S. A.	COLUMBIA		
TUCH FABRIK WILHELM BECKER	GERMANY	TEXTILES	15.00
SVENSKA PETROLEUM EXPLORATION AB	SWEDEN	OIL PROCESSING	14.36
CARGILL INC.	USA	CHEMICALS	14.30
SIEMENS AG	GERMANY	ELECTRONICS	13.83

Source: Lithuanian Development Agency

EDUCATION
AND SCIENCE

During the pre-war period (1918–1940), Lithuania was obliged to build the framework of a new educational system in place of the model it inherited from the Tsarist Empire. Education had been relatively neglected before the First World War. In 1913, only 875 primary-level schools were functioning, attended by 51,221 students. The total number of available teachers was a mere 1,022. As the school system expanded, Lithuanian educators increasingly relied on Western European models of education and pedagogical thought; this trend accelerated as contacts with Western Europe expanded.

In 1919, Lithuania started with 1,036 primary schools, 1,232 teachers and 45,540 students. By 1938, the number of these schools had more than doubled to 2,319. That same year there were already 5,110 teachers providing basic education to 283,773 students, or six times the number in 1919.

Secondary and higher education also developed rapidly. To meet Lithuania's modernisation needs, a new university was founded in Kaunas in 1922. Later, ten more higher education institutions were established.

The development of the education system, however, was interrupted by the Second World War and then adversely affected by the Soviet occupation. Although the number of people provided with education continued rising in the Soviet era, the educational system was reshaped according to Soviet norms. Nevertheless, the basic language of instruction was Lithuanian, although the Soviet authorities pressured Lithuania to increase the use of Russian.

EDUCATIONAL REFORM

Reforms of the education system started in 1988 and focused on the promotion of national, democratic and humanistic values.

Lithuania passed the Law on Academic Affairs and Studies in early 1991. Its main provisions were supported by additional legislation. These acts laid the foundation for reforming the system of academic affairs.

An all-encompassing reform package was approved in 1992. It was aimed at improving the general education of the personality, the development of communication skills, independent decision making, critical thinking, and informational and social skills. It intended to achieve a wider variety in the education system by increasing the diversity of educational institutions. Private educational institutions were established alongside state schools. Educational institutions run by religious denominations appeared. New educational institutions for ethnic minorities were established to provide better guarantees of minority cultural rights. Also, alternative approaches to teaching theory are being introduced.

PRE-SCHOOL EDUCATION

During the interwar era the majority of pre-school children were traditionally looked after at home. Soviet rule, however, changed this custom dramatically. The primary duty to provide children's education was taken over by the state. The highest number of pre-school educational institutions was attained in 1990 (a total of 1,681). More than half of these were located in rural areas.

The reestablishment of independence brought with it a change in emphasis towards the promotion of traditional values and the fostering of personal development. In 1997 there were 724 pre-school educational institutions, attended by 96,000 children. Of these, 90% were for children of three and over. They were staffed by a total of 12,200 teachers, almost entirely women. A total of 91% of these were graduates of higher education institutions.

The most popular types of pre-school educational institutions include crèches, crèche-kindergartens, kindergartens, kindergarten-schools and newly founded centres of pre-school education for handicapped children.

The Law on Education provides for the education of non-Lithuanian children in their native language, from the kindergarten to the higher education levels. A few kindergartens run by religious communities also exist.

PRIMARY AND SECONDARY EDUCATION

The current system consists of primary schools (1st–4th years), middle schools (5th–9th years), schools of general education (1st–12th years), gymnasiums (four years, equivalent to the 9th–12th years at the schools of general education), special educational institutions for handicapped children, schools for children offering basic education, educational institutions for adults (centres, adult groups in secondary schools, etc.), and secondary education in some higher schools. A new general education structure (4+6+2) will be introduced in the year 2000.

At the beginning of 1999 there were 2,352 general education schools, which were attended by 579,106 pupils.

In 1993 the first schools were established for children who lack motivation or cannot adjust to normal school conditions. There are 22 schools of this type.

Lithuania has 71 gymnasiums, and 18 secondary schools aspiring to gymnasium status. Vilnius has one internationally recognised International Baccalaureate school.

Education is compulsory for children until the age of 16. The

*THE CHILDREN'S TV SONG COMPETITION **DAINŲ DAINELĖ** HAS BEEN HELD ANNUALLY SINCE 1974*

reestablishment of gymnasiums was significant for improving pre-university education. Older pupils are usually divided into two groups, humanitarian and sciences. Unlike previous practice, all children, including the handicapped, are encouraged to deal with intellectual challenges. Many such children eventually transfer to regular schools.

Children belonging to ethnic minorities, notably Polish and Russian, have similar educational conditions to Lithuanian children. There are ethnic minority schools where the language of instruction is Russian, Polish, Yiddish, German and Belarusian. Ethnic minority study groups also exist at institutions of higher education.

THE TRAINING OF TEACHERS

Qualified teachers undergo vocational training at the Teacher In-service Training Institute (about 20,000 teachers a year). There are also more than 30 regional education centres offering in-service training, as well as similar centres at universities. A total of 85.5% of teachers are graduates of higher education institutions; about 10% of teachers have studied at specialised high schools. Teachers' professional qualifications are assessed regularly by special commissions. According to current regulations, all teachers have to undergo an appraisal every five years, during which their existing qualification category is confirmed or a higher one awarded. There are four major qualification categories: teacher, senior teacher, teacher-methodologist and expert teacher.

VOCATIONAL EDUCATION

There are 107 state, and one private, schools of vocational education, attended by a total of 52,000 students. The education in these schools lasts from two to four years. Students must be 14 and over to qualify. Education in technical schools is divided into four stages, which allows the students to choose courses according to their level.

New teaching programmes are being developed with the assistance of foreign experts. There are 11 priority areas of education which are to be reformed as soon as possible by the Phare-financed Vocational Education and Training Programme, which started in 1994. Altogether, 27 schools of vocational education participate in the project: they work with improved or newly created teaching programmes that comply with EU standards.

The EU Leonardo da Vinci programme offers institutions involved in vocational training support in their work. In 1997 a foundation was established in Lithuania to coordinate the programme. Since November 1998 the country has participated in the programme as an equal member.

In order to involve social partners in the activities of schools of vocational education, a tripartite Council for Lithuanian Vocational Education has been established. It is an advisory body that deals with issues of professional training. Bodies representing employers carry out an evaluation of new teaching programmes, and participate in the work of expert commissions. Since 1994, the skills of the graduates of schools of vocational education have been evaluated by the employers' commission.

COLLEGES

There are 68 higher schools in Lithuania. Higher school programmes are designed for pupils who already have a secondary education. The duration of courses is from three to four years. In 1997–1998 there were about 29,000 individuals pursuing studies in these schools. Education in non-government-run higher schools is conducted on a fee-paying basis. The emphasis is on practical vocational training.

The higher schools see their future as part of the non-university higher education sector of the European Union, which is a part of the educational system independent of universities. The newly prepared Law on Higher Education and the White Paper on Professional Training provide for the creation of colleges, a new type of school which will offer a higher professional education.

ADULT EDUCATION

The formal education of adults encompasses general secondary, vocational, higher and university-level education run by the state or institutions approved by it. The diplomas and certificates issued by these institutions are recognised by the state. One of the main problems in the formal education of adults is the creation of programmes that match specific requirements. The first modules for general training have already been devised and approved.

The rest of the adult education system is informal. The Law

on Adult Informal Education was passed on 30 June 1998. Certificates are recognised by employers, their organisations and unions. There are 300 institutions of informal education. Most of them are private, and oriented towards people of all ages.

A flexible system for training employed people is extra-mural education, also known as distance learning. Modern distance learning centres are being established at Vilnius University and Kaunas Technological University. There is also a centre for extra-mural education, which co-ordinates the activities of distance learning centres and their development.

The number of students and institutions involved in adult education declined steadily until 1993. However, in 1994 the number of schools stabilised, and student enrollment started growing rapidly. Some institutions have become centres for adult training for general education as well as informal education. There are currently ten such centres in Lithuania.

Eight regional information centres for adult education exist in Lithuania. In 1991, the Lithuanian Association for Adult Education and the Foundation for the Lithuanian Language were established. These organisations distribute information about adult education, and initiate and carry out new programmes.

HIGHER EDUCATION

Currently there are 15 university-level schools in Lithuania, with 68,000 students. To qualify, applicants must have completed their secondary education in various fields. University-level institutions attract students not just from secondary schools but also gymnasiums and colleges. Courses are divided into two levels: a four-year Bachelor's programme and a two-year Master's programme.

University-level education has come closer to Western standards. In 1988–1989 there was only one university, in Vilnius; now universities exist in almost every large city. University-level vocational education is offered by four specialised universities, six academies and one institute.

The number of full-time students and graduates has increased considerably as new university-level institutions have been established (including Vytautas Magnus University, the Academy of Law, the Military Academy) which offer full-time studies only.

The number of students is relatively high. In 1996, there were 226 per 10,000 inhabitants.

The level of accomplishment of Lithuanian students is high. However, there is still a shortage of well-equipped laboratories, textbooks and related literature, and technical equipment (computers, copying machines, audio-visual equipment, etc.), which is taken for granted in most Western universities.

In 1997, almost 20,000 students were accepted with full state scholarships. Some are external students who partly cover their own tuition fees.

University-level schools enjoy a high degree of independence, and are financed by the state.

The university-level schools are being restructured, using funds received through various international programmes aimed at modernising study programmes, bringing them closer to European standards, encouraging student and academic staff exchanges, developing research, and improving the quality of studies in specific disciplines (management, economics, political science and foreign languages).

STUDENTS AT THE ŠIAULIAI PEDAGOGICAL UNIVERSITY

The Grand Courtyard of Vilnius University

The teaching of foreign languages is facilitated by the large number of foreign teachers who come under various state and private programmes. Lithuania also attracts students from other countries: in 1996–1997 there were 370 foreign students. One important programme is concerned with inviting foreign students of Lithuanian origin to study in Lithuania. Such studies are supported financially by the American Lithuanian Foundation. Lithuanian courses are taken by young people from Poland, Russia, Belarus, Iceland, Sweden, Finland, the USA, Great Britain, Hungary and other countries. A key function of Lithuanian university-level schools is the strengthening of the country's ethnic and cultural identity. During the 50 years of the Soviet occupation, university-level schools were centres for the preservation and development of the national culture.

RESEARCH

At the end of the 1980s Lithuania had 12 tertiary-level academic institutions and over 20 scientific research and experimental organisations, which together employed about 15,500 researchers. The Academy of Sciences consisted of 17 separate institutes,

173

with 2,000 academic staff. After the reestablishment of independence, the number of staff at research institutions decreased, since reforms and changing financing conditions encouraged staff to move to other areas. Scientific research and experimental work is currently carried out by approximately 10,000 scientists. About 6,800 of them work at eight universities and seven other institutions of higher education. There are 29 national institutes for scientific research in Lithuania.

Lithuania's potential is represented well by the distribution of academics across different fields. At the beginning of 1998 it was as follows (in per cent): agricultural sciences, 5.6; natural sciences, 20.2; humanities, 22.4; mathematics, 3.5; medicine, 9.1; social sciences, 16.9; engineering, 22; theology, 0.3. In 1991, 48% belonged to technical disciplines; whereas the humanities and social sciences constituted respectively 9.5% and 7.6%.

The country's potential today has formed over a number of decades and depends very much on the competence and management skills of leading academics.

The mathematicians of Vilnius University and the Institute of Mathematics and Informatics can claim considerable achievements in their fields, including work in the theory of probability (Jonas Kubilius and his assistants) and statistics.

Researchers in physics have investigated quantum theory. At the Institute of Physics, the foundations for a new field in physics – nuclear meteorology – have been laid.

New laser methods have been created for researching physics and biophysics. At Vilnius University there are several separate trends in quantum electronics research. The first is research on parametric light phenomena in crystals, the second on ultrafast photophysics phenomena in molecules and the third is the development of scientific laser devices (for example, the laser scalpel, the parametric tunable femtosecond laser). Lithuanian scientists invented an original laser spectrometer which measures ultrafast processes in molecules lasting less than one picosecond. Picosecond solid state lasers and parametric generators manufactured in Lithuania are currently being used in Germany, the USA, Japan, Sweden, Denmark, Israel and elsewhere. Lithuanian lasers are used in Japan's and Israel's nuclear energy research centres. Berkeley University in the US has acquired a picosecond laser to be used in chemistry research.

The Institute of Semiconductor Physics and Vilnius University carry out research into the various qualities of semiconductors and the interaction of materials with electromagnetic waves, and develop new equipment using semiconductors.

Research in chemistry is mostly in electrochemistry. Lithuanian scientists are working on the elaboration of the theory of electrolytic isolation and related technologies (in particular Professor Juozas Matulis and his students). Also, the problems of metal corrosion, the synthesis of organic combinations, and the chemistry of environmental science are under intensive study.

Biomedical research is carried out in a number of universities and institutes. The leading areas are in botany and zoology and the focus is on increasing biological resources and their productivity.

During the last two decades, attention to environmental problems and recreation has grown considerably, including research into the country's water and land eco-systems, ecological optimisation of the landscape, and the ecological challenges facing the Baltic coast. The results allow the measurement of the efficiency of eco-systems and chart their evolution.

Considerable achievements have been recorded in research into the country's geography and geology. New deposits of natural resources have been discovered, including crude oil and iron ore.

Vilnius University and scientific institutions specialising in biochemistry carry out research into the biochemical and genetic functioning of cells, genetic and cellular research into immunity mechanisms, and experiments in genetic engineering. The results of a national research programme, The Molecular Foundations of Biotechnology, are likely to be of crucial importance for biomedicine and agricultural technology.

In the field of medicine, cardiology, oncology and rheumatology attract the attention of numerous medical researchers. Lithuania's largest clinics perform complex surgery of the heart, blood vessels and kidneys, and their transplantation.

Major centres for engineering are Kaunas Technological University, Gediminas Technical University in Vilnius, and the Lithuanian Institute of Energy. A wide range of problems in mechanics, electrotechnics, radioelectronics and industrial technology are researched here. Researchers into the latest technologies are especially interested in research on vibrations.

The Lithuanian Institute of Energy estimates energy needs, and carries out research on the exchange of heat and hydrodynamics in energy equipment, the security of nuclear reactors and technologies for storing radioactive waste. Another area of activity at the institute is the creation of fire-resistant materials.

After the restoration of independence and subsequent changes in values, an urgent need for new research appeared in the humanities and social sciences. Economics, law, sociology, philosophy, history, literature, art history and pedagogics all need a fresh approach to their problems. The ideas of leading researchers await further elaboration, including those of the archaeologist Marija Gimbutienė, the linguist and semiotician Algirdas Julius Greimas, the management specialist Vytautas Andrius Graičiūnas, and other well-known Lithuanian scientists.

Over the last 20 years, co-operation with foreign research institutions has increased dramatically. Each scientific institution in Lithuania has co-operation agreements with foreign partners. The work covers a wide range of projects, ranging from study visits to joint research projects, publications and lectures. Many scientific institutions and individual scientists in Lithuania belong to international organisations, and participate in leading international programmes that finance research, such as Phare, Copernicus, Tempus, UNESCO, NATO, and the Council of Europe. Lithuania's scientific societies have also become associate members of their respective international organisations.

THE HISTORY OF SCIENCE AND RESEARCH IN LITHUANIA

The history of the sciences in Lithuania starts with the founding in 1579 of Vilnius University (Academia et Universitas Vilnensis), one of the oldest universities in Eastern Europe. This occurred at a time when the nation's economic life was improving, and Renaissance ideas and the Reformation were spreading across the country. Many eminent scholars worked at Vilnius University in areas such as mathematics, medicine, the humanities, the natural and social sciences. Most professors had studied at leading Western European universities. Many professors and graduates of Vilnius University were invited to work in academic institutions, both old and newly established, in Eastern Europe and Russia. In the middle of the 17th century, *Artis Magnae Artilleriae* (1650) by Kazimieras Simonavičius was published in many European countries. In it, Simonavičius, an expert in artillery, discussed the creation of rockets. His diagrams of multistage rockets even resemble modern designs.

In 1773 a group of Vilnius University scientists, led by the eminent astronomer Martynas Počobutas, decided to found a Lithuanian academy of sciences, an institution to encourage scientific research and its popularisation. The plans, however, failed due to subsequent wars. Vilnius University was enlarged in 1803. The number of departments grew to 32, in which 55 disciplines were taught. Engineering, the theory of probability, agriculture, statistics and diplomacy were added, and research in these areas increased. The university was quick to react to socio-economic trends in Western Europe and took them up enthusiastically. Theodor Grotus established a laboratory independent of the university and laid the foundations for the theory of electrolysis, and the inventor Aleksandras Griškevičius attempted tirelessly to fly on the steam-driven machine that he constructed himself.

Other scientists from Vilnius also contributed to the proliferation of geographic and scientific discoveries of the 19th century. Ignas Domeika, a graduate of Vilnius University, became a well-known researcher into the natural history and natural resources of Chile, and later was appointed rector of Santiago University. A

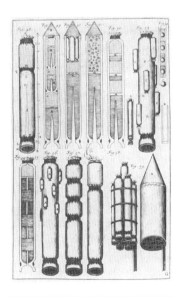

*SIMONAVIČIUS' DESIGNS FOR MULTI-STAGE ROCKETS (FROM **ARTIS MAGNAE ARTILLERIAE.** 1650)*

mountain in the Andes, a town (Puerto Domeika) and a mollusc were named after him.

Ivanas Čarskis, who graduated from the Vilnius Lyceum of the Nobility and was exiled from Lithuania, spent over a quarter of a century doing research on Lake Baikal in Siberia, and became a distinguished geologist, palaeontologist and geographer. His name was given to a mountain in Trans-Baikal and a group of mountains in northeast Siberia.

Tsarist Russia reacted to the popular uprising of 1831 with a vengeance: in 1832 Vilnius University was closed; in 1842 the Academy of Medical Surgery, the last institution of higher education in Lithuania, was also dissolved.

Nevertheless, the Lithuanian intelligentsia did not remain passive, channelling its energies towards more informal cooperation and association. Later, scientific societies were founded, including one of the first on the eastern coast of the USA in Baltimore in 1889. Another was established in Lithuania in 1907, and was active until 1940.

After the First World War, new scientific institutions in Lithuania were established or re-established. Vilnius University reopened, which led to successful research in mathematics, astronomy, the natural sciences and the humanities.

In 1920 an academy was founded in Kaunas, and in 1922 it was reorganised as Vytautas Magnus University. It subsequently became the main research centre in independent Lithuania. The university's geologists and mineralogists conducted extensive research on Lithuania's natural resources. Numerous volumes were published on geography, biology, medicine, mathematics, mechanics, physics and chemistry.

In the humanities the study of the Lithuanian language and culture prevailed, but there was also considerable research related to other countries and regions. Volumes on French and Russian literature were published. Levas Karsavinas, a historian and philosopher, wrote and published a five-volume *History of European Culture*. Considerable academic attention was devoted to the old Lithuanian Statute, a legal document of historical importance in Eastern Europe.

Alongside university studies, the Academy of Agriculture and an experimental agricultural station were established in Dotnuva. The botanist Dionizas Rudzinskas founded a laboratory in which he experimented on plant genetics and selection.

The idea of establishing an academy of sciences was not forgotten in independent Lithuania, but a lack of government financial support delayed the realisation of the undertaking. Only at the end of 1938 was the Institute of Lithuanian Studies founded, which was to develop into the multifaceted Academy of Sciences.

The 1940s were perhaps the most tragic period for academic life. Many leading scientists were killed or dispersed around the world. The work of the universities was discontinued because of the war and the Soviet and Nazi occupations. One date, however, was very positive for education and science. On 16 January 1941 the Lithuanian Academy of Sciences was formally established, although its individual branches were to be developed only after Lithuania started recovering from the devastation and disruptions of the war.

From the 1960s, most attention was paid to the natural sciences, physics and mathematics, leading to considerable achievements in these areas.

VILNIUS UNIVERSITY LASER CENTRE

HEALTH CARE
AND SOCIAL SECURITY

HEALTH CARE

In 1997 the Government proclaimed health care one of six priorities for state investment into the social sector. Of particular importance is the health of mothers and children. The implementation of the Mother and Child Health Programme has helped decrease the infant mortality rate from 16.4 in 1,000 live births in 1992, to 9.2 in 1998.

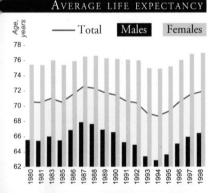

AVERAGE LIFE EXPECTANCY

Source: Lithuanian Department of Statistics

In addition new programmes aimed at combating cancer, cardiovascular diseases, diabetes, mental illness and suicide have been launched. The problem of integrating disabled people into society has received greater official and public attention.

In the area of environmental health, programmes for improving nutrition and food, and the hygiene of the work environment, are being developed.

Major areas of health policy include the Alcohol, Tobacco and Narcotics Control Programme, the social rehabilitation of drug addicts and imuno-prophylactics.

The Government investment programme includes assistance for the development of primary health care and disease prevention, the restructuring of the health care system, and the conservation of energy resources at hospital and clinic facilities.

In 1997, 4.2% of GDP was allocated for health care. In 1999

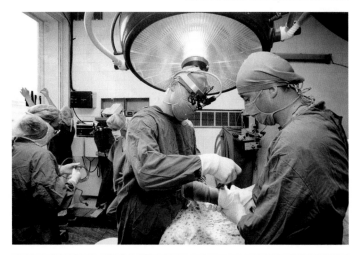

ABOUT 1,500 COMPLEX OPERATIONS ARE CARRIED OUT ANNUALLY AT THE PLASTIC AND RECONSTRUCTIVE MICROSURGERY DEPARTMENT OF VILNIUS UNIVERSITY RED CROSS HOSPITAL

this ratio rose to 4.9%. According to recent legislation on reform of the health care system, health care organisations have been reorganised into public enterprises. Administrative responsibility for the provision of public health services was delegated to three levels.

Local authorities are responsible for the organisation of primary medical services, which are provided by local health centres, polyclinics, first aid stations and other local health facilities.

Local and regional authorities are responsible for the second tier of medical services, namely more specialised health centres and medical services in hospitals.

The highest, tertiary, level of health care is concentrated at university clinics and institutions reporting directly to the Ministry of Health Care.

Medical practitioners are trained at three university-level academic institutions. Vilnius and Kaunas have university hospitals which combine research, training and patient care.

Lithuanian medical practitioners have received global recognition, particularly in the areas of cardiology, transplants, plastic reconstructive microsurgery, and neonatal treatment.

181

HEALTH CARE IN 1998

	No.	Per 10,000 pop.
Doctors	14,622	39.5
Dentists	2,259	6.1
Paramedic personnel	37,968	102.5
Pharmacists	2,146	5.8
Assistant pharmacists	1,834	5.0
Hospitals	187	–
Hospital beds	35,615	96.2

Heart and kidney transplants are conducted routinely. In the summer of 1999, Vilnius surgeons began performing the first successful heart bypass operations, which do not require artificial circulation of blood. Transplantations of bone marrow were begun in Vilnius in 1999.

A programme for developing the pharmaceutical industry is being developed. The country has 18 pharmaceutical enterprises, which produce over 800 types of

PRIVATE DENTAL CARE HAS MADE GREAT STRIDES RECENTLY

medicines. This covers a growing proportion of Lithuania's pharmaceutical needs.

The state encourages private medical practitioners, who are steadily expanding the range of their services. There are growing numbers of private dentists, surgeons, gynaecologists and family doctors. Private dentists already account for roughly one quarter of all Lithuanian dentists. As of the beginning of 1999, 271 private, non-dental health care facilities were in operation. In addition, 566 private dental clinics were registered and functioning. These private institutions were staffed by more than 1,500 doctors and dentists.

A number of well-equipped health complexes, including a large diagnostic centre, a reconstructive surgery clinic, several cardiac diagnosis facilities and a major dental clinic, have been operating in Vilnius for several years. These private sector institutions are equipped with the latest in Western technology, and are staffed by multilingual specialists trained in Western health facilities.

After the Law on Health Insurance was introduced, and health institutions were reorganised into public non-profit enterprises, ways have been sought to finance them through local patients' funds. For the time being, private practitioners are paid directly by their patients, and state medical institutions receive Government funds through local patients' funds.

SOCIAL POLICY

Since 1990 social policy in Lithuania has focused on two main areas: social security and employment. Employment policy is particularly concerned with the following: employment and the labour market, labour relations, and rates of pay. The social security system comprises social insurance and social assistance.

Social insurance is the largest part of the social security system. Employed and self-employed people are required to make pension contributions. Social security benefits are paid to retired people, the disabled, widows and orphans.

Retirement pensions consist of two parts: basic and supplementary parts. The amount of a basic pension does not depend on a person's former pay, but is determined by the Government. The basic pension offers minimum income guarantees and is linked to the retail price index. Persons having a minimum insurance period have the right to receive the full amount of the basic pension.

The supplementary pension depends on the former pay and the period of insurance. The indexing of this part of the pension is related to the average of the insured income.

Over the last two years, pensions grew more rapidly than the price index. In 1998, the basic retirement pension was 290 litas.

As in most European countries, Lithuanian society is growing older. In an attempt to counter the negative effects of society's ageing, in 1995 the retirement age was raised two months for men and four months for women. This periodic adjustment of the retirement age will continue until 2009, when women's retirement age will reach 60 and the retirement age for men will be 62.5.

Employed people who have sickness or maternity insurance receive sickness and maternity benefits. This amounts to 80% of pay for the first month of sickness and 100% for subsequent months.

Only employed and self-employed people have unemployment insurance. However, the right to receive unemployment benefits is also applied to individuals who have no insurance (for instance, graduates of higher education who are unable to find employment). Over the last year, unemployment benefits were paid on average to 22,000 people monthly.

SOCIAL ASSISTANCE AND SOCIAL SERVICES

Social assistance in cash in Lithuania is usually offered in the form of benefits. Some benefits are awarded to certain social groups regardless of income; others are offered only after verifying that the applicants or their family indeed have a low income. Most benefits come from regional budgets and are administered by the social assistance divisions of the municipalities.

The first group of benefits includes maternity/paternity and childcare benefits, as well as financial assistance to defray burial

POPULATION BY SEX
AND AGE IN 1998
(AS OF JANUARY 1)

Age, years

Males | Females

90+
85-89
80-84
75-79
70-74
65-69
60-64
55-59
50-54
45-49
40-44
35-39
30-34
25-29
20-24
15-19
10-14
5-9
0-4

Thous.

120 80 40 0   0 40 80 120 160

Source: Lithuanian Department of Statistics

costs. Childcare benefits are provided to families raising a child until 3 years of age for each child and to families which adopt and care for children. Beginning in 1997 large families (three and more children) have been receiving enlarged family benefits until the children reach 16 or, if they are full-time students, until they complete their studies. In order to receive an enlarged benefit, the family having 3 children is required to demonstrate that its total income is less than three minimum Family Support Incomes.

The second group of benefits includes social benefits to families earning less than the Family Support Income. Such families receive from the regional administration budget benefits which amount to 90% of the difference between this minimum income and their real income. Families with low incomes also receive state assistance to defray the costs of residential heating and hot and cold water. In 1998, this aid cost 150 million litas.

People who have never been employed because of disability, childcare responsibilities or their care for disabled people and are consequently not eligible for a social insurance pension, are still eligible for a relief pension. In 1998 this pension amounted to 138 to 207 litas and was paid to over 50,000 individuals.

In extreme circumstances – loss of home, loss of a job, disability, alcoholism, drug addiction or other problems – families and individuals receive social assistance. This is aimed at restoring the person's ability to take care of himself and live a full life in society.

The Law on Social Services, which came into force in autumn 1996, requires municipalities to offer general social services: providing information and consultations, assistance at home, nursing at home, and the provision of relief. These services help people by creating conditions allowing them to live at home in familiar surroundings. Only in cases where general social services are insufficient are people offered special social services such as day care, temporary housing or nursing services. Non-governmental organisations are increasingly involved in offering various social services.

EMPLOYMENT AND LABOUR MARKET POLICY

From 1991 to 1995 the number of people employed in all sectors of the economy decreased by 250,000, and it was only in 1996, when the economy started growing, that employment started increasing as well. According to the Lithuanian Labour Exchange, unemployment in 1998 was 6.4%.

Eligibility for unemployment benefits, the conditions for granting and paying benefits as well as their amount, are set out in the Law on the Support of the Unemployed. The size of benefits depends on the number of years the individual has had state social insurance and the reasons for unemployment. With some exceptions, the duration of unemployment benefits normally extends to six months. In 1998 average unemployment benefits amounted to 135 to 270 litas a month.

The priorities in labour market policy include the prevention of unemployment and the support and protection of employment. Special attention is devoted to the implementation of an active labour market policy to help unemployed individuals find permanent jobs.

Labour market policy is implemented through mediation, the organisation of vocational training, the support of employment (the organisation of public works through the Employment Fund, support for new businesses, creation of new jobs for socially disadvantaged people), and the development of local employment programmes.

In 1998 new administrative procedures were approved to expand the scope of public works. Public works may be organised in every enterprise or institution if they contribute to the development of the local social infrastructure.

Measures to improve young people's professional qualifications and their integration into the labour market are being implemented since the highest unemployment rates are among the unskilled. Attempts are being undertaken to provide vocational guidance and counseling for young people, increase their participation in vocational training programmes and facilitate their mobility.

In May of 1999, the average pre-tax monthly wage equalled USD 267. Although small, this figure has been growing steadily since the introduction of the litas in 1993. From 1993 to 1999, average wages measured in litas have increased 568% thanks to price stabilisation and growing output and productivity. Recently real wages have been rising over 27% per year. The most remunerative professional fields are banking, finance, government service, real estate and the energy sector. The least well-paid occupations are in the farming, forestry and hotel and restaurant sectors.

CULTURE

In 1997 Lithuania celebrated an important date – the 450th anniversary of the beginning of its literary tradition. The birth of the written language is a key event in any nation's public and cultural life, perhaps even a historical turning point. For Lithuania, this event was the appearance of the first Lithuanian book, Martynas Mažvydas' *Catechismus*, published in 1547 in Karaliaučius (Kaliningrad). The first steps in literature, as in most European countries, were related to religion. Lithuanian fiction, as an art form, belongs to the 19th century, especially to the second half of the century and the era of the national reawakening.

However, one leading light of the national literature originated in the 18th century: this was Kristijonas Donelaitis (1714–1780), a poet and the founder of Lithuanian letters. Donelaitis' poem *The Seasons*, published only in 1818, half a century after it was written, has been translated into many languages. The Lithuanians, although they have a vast number of folk songs and tales, do not have a national epic. *The Seasons*, a poetic encyclopaedia of the life of 18th-century serfs, compensates to some extent for this shortcoming.

THE FIRST LITHUANIAN BOOK, MAŽVYDAS' **CATECHISMUS**

187

M.K.Ciurlionis. The Kings

The period from the end of the 18th to the beginning of the 20th centuries was marked by the rule of the Russian Empire. Especially damaging was the ban on printing Lithuanian publications in the Roman script from 1863 to 1904. To circumvent this prohibition publishers had books printed in neighbouring East Prussia and smuggled across the border. The book smugglers risked long terms of hard labour in Siberia.

During this difficult period, there emerged only a few exceptionally gifted poets, such as Antanas Baranauskas and Maironis, who found some protection from the secular authorities by virtue of their senior positions in the clergy. Baranauskas' poem *The Forest of Anykščiai* and Maironis' collection of verses *The Voices of Spring* consistently appear in anthologies of Lithuanian literature. In 1898, Vincas Kudirka wrote *Tautinė giesmė* (The National Song), which is the national anthem of Lithuania today.

At the turn of the 20th century, Lithuanian literature was enriched by many distinguished authors who, through their books and periodicals, prepared the country for independence. Within the space of a few decades, they took up the experience of the great European literary tradi-tions, and at an accelerated rate, embarked on the search for modernist forms. Regrettably, very few of their works are available in English.

Among the outstanding literary figures of this period are: Žemaitė, the founder of Lithuanian realist prose; Jonas Biliūnas, a master of the psychological novel; Juozas Tumas-Vaižgantas and Vincas Krėvė, pioneers of patriotic writing; Vincas Myko-laitis-Putinas, a gifted poet, writer and academic; and Balys Sruoga, a poet, prose writer and playwright (his memoirs about the Stuthoff concentration camp appeared under the title *Forest of the Gods*).

Independence and the Devastation of the Second World War

The two decades of independence, ending in the tragic year of 1940, provided a new generation of writers with the opportunity to mature in a Lithuania free of foreign domination.

The Lithuanians tend to consider themselves a lyrical and poetic nation, and foreigners familiar with the Lithuanian character usually agree. Among the most visible representatives of Lithuanian poetry are Jonas Aistis (1904–1973), Bernardas Brazdžionis (born 1907), Antanas Miškinis (1905–1983) and Salomėja Nėris (1904–1945): colourful and creative personalities who belong to the neo-Romantic generation.

Their fates, however, were strikingly different. Aistis and Brazdžionis fled the approaching second Soviet occupation in the summer of 1944. Miškinis spent a decade of torture in Siberian concentration camps for participating in the resistance. Nėris, the greatest Lithuanian poetess, was entangled in the political intrigues of 1940. She and her young child were evacuated to the Soviet Union during the war.

Petras Cvirka, another active writer of the period, experienced a fate similar to Nėris'. Cvirka and Nėris, although labelled as Soviet classics, produced their most mature works during the period of independence. Nėris' lyrical collection *I'll Blossom in Absinthe* (1938) earned her the National Prize. Cvirka's children's stories *Sugar Lambs*, and the collection *Daily Stories* (1938), which followed in the tradition of Guy de Maupassant and Anton Chekhov, are two works of quite different genres.

In 1944, almost 70% of the members of the Lithuanian Writers Union chose exile rather than "Stalin's sunshine". Many of the writers who stayed in Lithuania followed in the footsteps of the writer Miškinis. Scores of young and promising writers perished in the armed resistance or the cold of Siberian labour camps. It was only after independence was reestablished in 1990 that the formerly banned works of deportees and partisans, such as Miškinis' *Broken Crosses* and Kazys Inčiūra's *The Psalms of Captivity,* were published.

From the perspective of the present day, the devastation of the 1940s and 1950s resembles that of a natural disaster. Only recently has the emptiness of this period been filled by emigre literature, which has been returning to Lithuania. Emigre writers saved and ensured the continuity of Lithuanian literature; they also enriched it by using the experience of the Western literary tradition.

Emigre Writers in the West
Overcoming considerable material and psychological difficulties, these emigre writers persevered as creative personalities far away from their native land. They, as well as a new generation of writers who matured in the West, synthesised the creative spirit of the free world with the despair and loss of their native land.

Special mention ought to be made of the exile poets who were designated the *žemininkai*, a name that comes from their anthology *Žemė* (The Soil), published in Chicago in 1951. This generation of poets was born in the 1920s and includes Henrikas Radauskas, Kazys Bradūnas, Henrikas Nagys and Alfonsas Nyka-Niliūnas.

Two different genres of literature – traditional prose and stream of consciousness – are represented by two leading emigre writers, Marius Katiliškis (*Shelter, Autumn Comes Through the Woods, Gone Never to Return*) and Antanas Škėma (*The White Shroud*). In the last decade all of them returned to Lithuania, either figuratively or literally. Some came to spend the autumn of their lives in their native land (Bradūnas); the ashes of some were returned to their motherland (Krėvė, Nagys); and still others, after years of exile, were finally published in Lithuania.

The Khrushchev Thaw and Beyond

Emigre literature, however, did not return to a vacuum. The end of the 1950s and the so-called Khrushchev thaw finally provided Lithuanian literature some scope for genuine expression. Although

constrained by censorship and the concept of Socialist Realism, Lithuanian literature managed to escape becoming an unconditional servant of the oppressive ideology.

Poetry was especially well suited to circumvent the demands of official ideology. Initially it managed to defend its natural right to an individual and lyrical concept of the world; later it elaborated a cryptic language that was more understandable to the reader than to official censors. On the other side of the Iron Curtain, Eduardas Mieželaitis, a contemporary of the *žemininkai* generation, achieved renown for his innovations. Justinas Marcinkevičius and Algimantas Baltakis have earned a well-deserved reputation for continuing Lithuanian poetic traditions from the 1960s to the present.

The brightest and the most original names that have caught the attention of contemporary readers are Vytautas Bložė, Sigitas Geda, Marcelijus Martinaitis, Jonas Strielkūnas, Judita Vaičiūnaitė, Onė Baliukonytė, Gintaras Patackas and others. Having established their own poetic idiom, they also belong to the modern European poetic tradition. One might argue that, because of their unique experience, their

THE POETRY SPRING FESTIVAL IS HELD ANNUALLY

poetry is somewhat more painful, deeper, more multifaceted and marked with bright national colours.

The Soviet years were more challenging and damaging for prose. It was more prone to official taboos, political and ideological directives, and official lies. These years are marked by the avoidance of certain historical periods, important subjects and problems, and an understated language of allusions and codes. These tendencies to avoid and distort truth were especially damaging, since the reading public expected major works to address the profound issues of private or public life.

Smaller works were in a better position, since they attracted less attention from the authorities. Their authors were able to deal with universal ethical or existential problems. But even these writers were accused of being too pessimistic, nostalgic, and lacking relevant, that is, socialist, subject matter. However, in spite of these shortcomings, prose played an important role in the country's cultural and spiritual life. The suggestive power, maturity, and authenticity of their characters permitted Lithuanian prose writers to produce works that even today powerfully reflect the spirit of this period. The best works of Juozas Aputis, Jonas Avyžius, Vytautas Bubnys, Vytautas Martinkus and Jonas Mikelinskas are still relevant today and bear witness to the historical and spiritual experience as well as the aspirations of the Lithuanian people and the individual.

Drama occupies a special place in the nation's spiritual life. Historical dramas by Juozas Grušas (*Herkus Mantas*, *Barbora Radvilaitė*) and Justinas Marcinkevičius (*Mindaugas*, *Mažvydas*, *Cathedral*); grotesque dramas and tragi-comedies by Kazys Saja (*Mammoth Hunting*) and Juozas Glinskis (*The House of Correction*); Saulius Šaltenis' plays, lyrical and full of irony, formed the Lithuanian national theatre. They sometimes became a potent public voice which attracted close surveillance by the ideological masters.

Lithuania boasts a rich children's literature in which the poetised daily reality that surrounds the young reader is matched by rich fantasy, romantic adventures and subtle humour. The poets Martynas Vainilaitis and Ramutė Skučaitė, the writers Kazys Saja, Vytautas Petkevičius, Vytautas Račickas, Vytautė Žilinskaitė, and the playwright Violeta Palčinskaitė are just a few of the names that represent the scale of creative individuality and the variety of genres.

National and personal experiences, suppressed for decades, today emerge with all their historical uniqueness in post-modern forms. Popular, shocking and controversial, Ričardas Gavelis (the novel *Vilniaus pokeris*) and Jurgis Kunčinas (*Tūla*) are at least two writers that represent this tendency well.

The search for artistic truth has always been a test for both the author and his work. This is the process that Lithuanian writers are going through today.

FINE ARTS

The oldest pieces of art discovered in Lithuania date back to the third millennium BC. These are little sculptures and amulets made of amber, wood and bone, weapons and jewellery, and other decorated handicrafts made out of ivory, horn or wood. According to archaeological evidence, Lithuanians in the tenth century were making pottery, decorated weapons, and a vast range of fashion accessories, including metal-decorated hats, belts, brooches, etc. Since the 13th century the production of decorative items was influenced by Western European trends. The surviving decorations of the Laurušavas Gospel are a witness to Byzantine influence. After adopting Christianity, the development of the fine arts in the Grand Duchy of Lithuania was closely related to religious art. Objects of art were frequently made by Western European artists who were invited to the Lithuanian court and estates via Poland, as well as by anonymous local artists.

An important place in the fine arts tradition belongs to the portraits of the nobility and senior clergy. Copies of Latin and Slavonic manuscripts with painted illuminations have survived, as have fragments of wall paintings located in the crypt of Vilnius Cathedral. The Chodkevičius Palace in Vilnius, with its extensive collection of paintings, provides a good overview of the history of Lithuanian art up to the end of the 19th century.

Another important aspect of Lithuanian art is represented by its churches. Vilnius is a Baroque city, as the architecture and art of this style had a very strong impact on Lithuanian culture and acquired some specific local features. Lithuanian Baroque has been attracting growing interest, especially after the country joined the international Baroque Road programme, initiated by the Council of Europe. In the framework of this programme a series of exhibitions was held over several years (Baroque Art in Lithuania, in 1996 and 1997, and the Monasteries of Lithuania, in 1998). This was the first opportunity for the public to learn about Lithuanian religious painting, sculpture and applied art of the 17th and 18th centuries.

One of the most important examples of Baroque sculpture is the interior of St Peter and Paul's Church, which was designed by the Italian sculptors P. Perti and G.M. Galli, with the assistance of local craftsmen.

The heritage of applied Baroque art is much more extensive, since church liturgy and practices required extravagant robes, tapestries, wood carvings, metalwork, and items of gold and silver. In 1998 the public learned for the first time about the treasures of church art hidden in the crypt of Vilnius Cathedral.

The professional fine arts in Lithuania date back to 1793, when the Architecture Department was established at Vilnius University. It was headed by Laurynas Stuoka-Gucevičius, the first exponent of Classicism in Lithuanian architecture. The first professor of the Department of Drawing and Painting (established in 1797) was Pranciškus Smuglevičius, who had studied in Warsaw and Rome. Thanks to Smuglevičius, the Vilnius Art School became a leading artistic centre in Lithuania and Poland. Later, the Department of Painting was headed by the professor and well-known portrait painter Jonas Rustemas. Rustemas' work and teaching in the early 19th century had an enormous impact on the development of Lithuanian painting.

At the beginning of the 20th century artists were faced with the challenge of creating a new national art responding to national cultural needs. The Lithuanian Art Society was established in 1907, and by 1914 had organised its first exhibitions of professional and folk art. The first Lithuanian art exhibition, which also included works of folk art, was held in Vilnius at the beginning of 1907. In other exhibitions in the early 20th century such a combination of professional and folk art became a tradition and even took on an ideological importance.

M.K. Čiurlionis

A special case at the beginning of the 20th century was the painter and composer Mikalojus Konstantinas Čiurlionis (1875–1911). His uniqueness has hardly any parallels in Lithuanian art, although he was not isolated from the artistic currents of the time. The work of this gifted artist embraced Symbolism and Romanticism.

Čiurlionis studied in Warsaw and Leipzig, participated in or-

ganising the Lithuanian Art Society, led a choir, gave piano recitals, and wrote on issues of art and music. The early works of Čiurlionis deal with cosmogony, and religious, historiosophic, psychological and symbolic themes, as well as musical allusions.

Most of his early works are imaginary or allegorical landscapes, and are clearly related to Symbolism. Almost all of his early creations were done in pastels. The artist was especially fond of painting cycles, which were given the structure of musical compositions (sonata, prelude, fugue).

The most important period of his work is 1907 to 1909, which coincided with a shift in emphasis from pastel to tempera. Čiurlionis' work of this period reflects a diversity of themes and artistic images, the artist's interest in the hermetic aspects of nature and the universe, and existential problems (the paintings *Rex, Hymn, Offering,* and the cycles *Winter, Spring, Summer, Zodiac,* etc.). The art of Čiurlionis never lost its connection with the national traditions of lyrical and romantic art.

Art in Independent Lithuania

The 20 years of independence were extremely diverse with regard to artistic movements. The

Lithuanian Society of Artists was established in Kaunas in 1920. Another important event was the opening of the Čiurlionis Art Gallery in Kaunas in 1925. It housed the works of Čiurlionis as well as a collection of professional and folk art.

The 1920s witnessed the birth of a new generation which challenged the old values of realism, academism and naturalism, and attempted to enrich the somewhat provincial Lithuanian artistic tradition with fresh ideas. Most artists of the new generation graduated from Kaunas Art School, and later continued their studies in Western Europe under distinguished artists such as Bourdelle, Despiau, Léger and others. This generation includes artists who belonged to the Society of Independent Artists and the Ars group of the early 1930s.

In the sculpture of the period, along with the prevailing realism (Juozas Zikaras, Vincas Grybas), new and fresh tendencies also appeared. Juozas Mikėnas, Bronius Pundzius, Robertas Antinis and Petras Aleksandravičius took over from their instructors in Paris the concept of monumen-

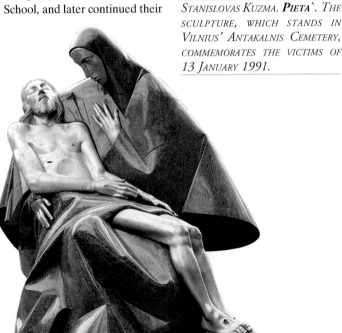

*STANISLOVAS KUZMA. **PIETA`**. THE SCULPTURE, WHICH STANDS IN VILNIUS' ANTAKALNIS CEMETERY, COMMEMORATES THE VICTIMS OF 13 JANUARY 1991.*

tal and laconic forms. Professional sculpture of that time drew strong visual and conceptual influences from folk art. Expressionist tendencies influenced a few sculptors. The most important exponent of this tradition was Matas Menčinskas, who did not follow other Lithuanian artists to Paris, preferring instead studies in Madrid and later in Buenos Aires.

Lithuanian art in 1940 and 1941 experienced numerous losses, since a large part of the intelligentsia, including many distinguished artists, fled the Soviet occupation of Lithuania.

After the war, the centre of cultural life moved from Kaunas to Vilnius, which became the home for the reopened Vilnius Art School. The Society of Arts also moved to Vilnius in 1944.

Painting became more figurative, with landscapes, still lifes and portraits prevailing. The development of sculpture was limited due to materials shortages. One exception, however, was Bronius Pundzius' relief on the Puntukas stone commemorating the heroic deeds of the pilots Darius and Girėnas.

The 1950s and After

The modern era in Lithuanian art coincided with the period of relative liberalisation of the 1950s in the Soviet Union. As public life grew more open, there was an opportunity to reconsider the values of the national artistic heritage, the traditions developed by artists of different generations, and the artists who had been undeservedly isolated from public life on account of ideological reasons. Painting increasingly dealt with monumental and laconic images as well as expressive forms.

Graphic art of the 1950s and 1960s was marked by interpretations of folk art traditions based on metaphorical representations, decorative qualities, and laconic means of expression. The works of Lithuanian graphic artists were praised in world book illustration forums. Of note were the works of Algirdas Steponavičius and Birutė Žilytė, who were awarded the Golden Apple prize in Bratislava. The works of the graphic artists Vytautas Kalinauskas, Rimtautas Gibavičius and Stasys Krasauskas enjoyed great popularity at the time.

Sculpture was dominated by monuments (Bronius Vyšniauskas, Gediminas Jokūbonis, Konstantinas Bogdanas), which relied on state commissions. The younger generation preferred smaller sculptures, interpreting the traditions of old Lithuanian sculpture, transforming forms and combining Constructivism with decoration.

After the reestablishment of independence, the public learnt about Silent Modernism, unofficial art which had existed and developed along with the official "achievements of Soviet Lithuanian Art". The book *Silent Modernism: 1962–1982* by Elona Lubytė added more clarity to the balance between official art and individual private work during the Soviet occupation. These attempts, limited as they were, contributed to the preservation and development of the national identity.

The work of Šarūnas Sauka is somewhat distant from the mainstream of Lithuanian painting. He was awarded the first National Prize in independent Lithuania. Sauka creates strong impressions through mysterious images, deep metaphors and dreams. His art is marked with the dialectics of beauty and ugliness, spirituality and decay.

An exceptional figure in the graphic arts of the last decades is Petras Repšys. His frescoes in Vilnius University have become a significant expression of Baltic culture, covering the mythological, historical and mundane aspects of that tradition. Repšys'

medals have earned him a strong reputation among European miniature artists. His etchings – for which he was awarded the National Prize – occupy a very special place in the tradition of Lithuanian graphic art.

The last decade of the 20th century is marked by the rapid change of artistic criteria and means of expression. During this decade of independence, the work of art institutions has changed dramatically. Along with state-owned galleries, dynamic private galleries have appeared. New trends and modernist forms of artistic language were facilitated

STASYS KRASAUSKAS.
BOOK ILUSTRATION. LINOCUT

by the opening of the Vilnius Contemporary Arts Centre in 1992 and, slightly later, the Soros Contemporary Arts Centre.

THEATRE

In an attempt to evade Tsarist Russian oppression in the 19th century, theatre lovers began to organise clandestine theatrical productions in remote areas of the countryside. Secret performances were often held in barns or large village houses. These were gatherings of amateurs, who included in their programmes po-

PETRAS REPŠYS. *THE SEASONS* (DETAIL). *THE FRESCO WAS COMPLETED FOR THE 400-YEAR ANNIVERSARY OF VILNIUS UNIVERSITY*

etry readings, dances, games and usually a short play. The initiators of these evenings were members of the intelligentsia: priests, teachers, doctors, lawyers, and students studying at Moscow or St Petersburg. Many of the actors were ordinary village people with-

out any training or experience. Balys Sruoga, a leading theatre historian, called this symbiosis a "fusion of university and black-soil natures". These secret theatre performances started in 1885 and rapidly became very popular across the whole of Lithuania (in spite of their strict prohibition by the Tsarist administration).

After the Tsarist regime was forced to repeal the prohibition of the Latin alphabet in 1904, these clandestine evening performances ended their noble mission. They were replaced by cultural societies, which appeared in the towns or large villages. These societies, choirs, dance and drama groups brought together the emerging intelligentsia and helped to develop its national consciousness. Amateur theatres were influenced by the experience of foreign professional theatre. Most leading future playwrights, directors and actors started their careers in the cultural society theatres.

The restoration of the country's statehood in 1918 was a powerful impetus for the development of Lithuanian culture generally and the theatre in particular. The Society of Lithuanian Artists, which was established in Kaunas, the interim capital, gave

birth to the first cultural institutions: the Art School, the Conservatoire and the theatre. Lithuania welcomed back a number of actors who had formerly worked in Russian theatres. Young directors, such as Antanas Sutkus and Borisas Dauguvietis, who were to play a significant role later, returned to Lithuania after completing their theatre studies in Russia. All of them created and worked in the first professional Lithuanian theatre in Kaunas. The first historical premiere, *St John's Day* by Zudermann, took place on 19 December 1920.

Lithuanian opera was led by Kipras Petrauskas, an eminent tenor, who had left the well-known Mary Theatre in St Petersburg to join the Lithuanian Opera Theatre. The first decade of independence was marked by an impressive number of premieres. As many as 13 would be staged each season.

In 1929 the State Theatre was headed by Andrius Oleka-Žilinskas, a disciple of Stanislavski, who, after graduating from the First Moscow Theatre Art Studio, was engaged as an actor at the famous Second Moscow Art Theatre. Oleka-Žilinskas was to become a leading director, achieving impressive results with his professionally trained group. He directed Vincas Krėvė's *Šarūnas*,

Charles Dickens' *The Chimes*, and Balys Sruoga's *The Giant's Shadow*.

From 1885 to 1940 Lithuanian theatre underwent stages of development which other theatre traditions experienced in several centuries.

Lithuanian theatre was strongly influenced by Mikhail Chekhov, a gifted Russian actor, teacher, director and disciple of Stanislavski, who spent several seasons working at the State Theatre and thereby gave this institution a strong and invigorating dose of the Stanislavski system.

By 1940 a young generation of directors was ready to make its mark on Lithuanian theatre. This generation included Romualdas Juknevičius and Algirdas Jakše-vičius, two gifted disciples of Oleka-Žilinskas. The two decades of independence also fostered a large group of talented actors, including Ona Rymaitė, Petras Kubertavičius, Ona Kurmytė and others. It gave new life to the plays of Balys Sruoga, Vincas Krėvė, Kazys Binkis, Vincas Mykolaitis-Putinas and Maironis, and formed a distinctive tradition of poetic realism, psychological depth, and fidelity to the truth.

The Soviet occupation from 1945 to 1990 was a period of unprecedented ideological pressure and suppression for the national theatre. Directors would lose their jobs, be exiled or even subjected to unconcealed oppression. The theatre was obliged to deal with the theory of "the absence of conflict," as well as periods of ideological "freezes" and "thaws". Soviet plays constituted almost half of the repertoires. Still, the theatre resisted the Soviet system during those grim years.

This self-assertion grew visibly stronger from 1970 when Lithuanian history was brought back to the stage. The poet Justinas Marcinkevičius wrote his well-known trilogy, *Mindaugas*, *Cathedral* and *Mažvydas*. These historically based plays brought a breath of fresh air to the theatre and strengthened national feelings. The plays of the directors Henrikas Vancevičius, Jonas Jurašas and Vytautas Čibiras challenged the regime and Soviet ideology. The theatre was a leading field in developing an allegorical language to communicate prohibited truths by hints and allusions.

During that period innovative plays were directed by Juozas Miltinis, a disciple of Charles Dulan, a leading reformer in French theatre. Among these were Miller's *Death of a Salesman*, Strindberg's *The Dance of Death*, and Dürrenmatt's *The Physicists*. These philosophical and intellectual works contributed considerably to the reputation of Lithuanian theatre.

The young director Dalia Tamulevičiūtė revived the Youth Theatre and brought to it some of her gifted students in 1974, including Eimuntas Nekrošius. Nekrošius later directed a series of plays which earned him his reputation as one of Lithuania's premier directors. These included *Pirosmani, Pirosmani*, Aitmatov's *And Longer Than a Century Lasts the Day*, Chekhov's *Uncle Vanya*, and the Shakespeare-based *Love and Death in Verona*. Shakespeare's *Hamlet* and *Macbeth* travelled to many foreign theatres and earned awards at prestigious international festivals. Nekrošius belongs to the Lithuanian and the world stage, and continues to amaze the public with his talent, originality and uncommon ability to free the actor's spirit.

The Lithuanian theatre has no shortage of gifted directors. Another successful modern director is Rimas Tuminas. His plays have been widely acclaimed abroad. Jonas Vaitkus, Oskaras Koršunovas, and the young Gintaras Varnas are other leading names among gifted directors who are active in the Lithuanian theatre.

FILM

Many critics trace the beginning of Lithuanian film to 1909, when Vladislovas Starevičius shot his now lost *Prie Nemuno* (Near the Nemunas River). Starevičius produced cartoons, *The Beautiful Lukanidė* and *The Ant and the Grasshopper*. But a Lithuanian-American, Antanas Račiūnas, who arrived in Lithuania the same year and began making films for export to the Lithuanian community abroad, is also considered a founder of Lithuanian cinema.

During the interwar years newsreels became popular. Two film companies, *Lietfilmas* and *Akis*, were established in Kaunas during the second half of the 1920s. The *Akis* company made the first feature films, *The Doctor in Spite of Himself* (1927) and *Onytė and Jonelis* (1931).

During the Soviet period about four feature films and 30 documentary films were produced each year, although many of them were propagandistic in nature. This pattern continued until 1990. Nevertheless, some Lithuanian films were recognised in international festivals for their artisitc qualities. Arūnas Žebriūnas' *The Last Day of the Holidays* (1964) was awarded a prize at the 1965 Locarno Festival and the 1966 Cannes Festival.

In the late 1980s Lithuanian film found a new life and played an important role in encouraging the country's drive for independence. Several independent film studios were established, such as the Kinema studio founded by the young director Šarūnas Bartas. With the restoration of independence, however, government funding decreased and costs of filmmaking rose dramatically. At the same time, the former production and distribution channels were replaced by an onslaught of imports from Hollywood and Western Europe.

Despite the economic burdens, Lithuanian film has survived and is beginning to flourish again. Andrius Stony's film *Neregių žemė* (The Land of the Blind) was awarded the Felix for Best Documentary by the European Academy of Film, and Šarūnas Bartas' *Trys dienos* (Three Days), produced by the Kinema studio, was nominated for Best Young Director. He has had more recent works screened in the Certain Regard Section of the Cannes Festival since then. Documentary films by Andrius Stonys and Arūnas Matelis have been screened at some of the largest festivals around the world. In 1998, the film *Vilko dantų karoliai* (The Necklace of Wolf's Teeth) by Algimantas Puipa, based on the novel of the same name by the painter and writer Leonardas

Gutauskas, won the top prize at the Stockholm Film Festival.

PHOTOGRAPHY

Lithuanian photography was born in the interwar years, during which it quickly took on the features that have prevailed until today: highly-personalised, realistic and sensitive depictions of daily life. But the real growth of the art of photography in Lithuania came in the 1950s and 1960s.

Vytautas Stanionis was the leading post-war photographer, and his realism earned him wide respect. In the 1960s younger photographers such as Antanas Sutkus, Aleksandras Macijauskas, Algimantas Kunčius and

Romualdas Rakauskas introduced a strong aspect of intimacy, deep psychological insight and personality into the impersonal and ideological photographic scene in the Soviet Union. Lithuanian photography became a not so subtle form of social criticism: doubtful of progress, focusing on the mundane rather than

VITALIJUS BUTYRINAS, FROM THE SERIES **TALES OF THE SEA**

the romanticised. Antanas Sutkus has won many of the top prizes in international competitions and has exhibited all over the world.

In the 1970s and 1980s, a new generation of photographers continued to break taboos and push the boundaries of their discipline. Photographers like Vytas Luckus and Romualdas Požerskis focused their lenses on the darker sides of life. They explored themes like the lives of the mentally handicapped and disabled, alcoholism and even the lives of exiles and political prisoners. Photographers were never more popular, as they were powerful voices of social criticism and political expression in Lithuania.

The newest generation of Lithuanian photographers has turned to subjectivism and more abstract forms of expression. Stanislovas Žvirgždas, Vitalijus Butyrinas, Algimantas Aleksandravičius and Romualdas Požerskis have trained their cameras on objects of daily life and the human body.

What was once more or less a single school of photography has grown into a diverse range of traditional and experimental work, both incorporating and opposing foreign trends.

MUSIC

Modern Lithuanian music starts with the work of Mikalojus Konstantinas Čiurlionis (1875–1911). The works of this patriarch of Lithuanian music consist of symphonic music (the symphonic poems *In the Forest* and *The Sea*) and compositions for piano, which are typical of the European music of the early 20th century: late Romanticism is transformed into Expressionist and Constructivist forms. Many later composers developed Čiurlionis' key concept that Lithuanian music rests on a synthesis of folk music and modern European forms of musical expression.

The years of independence were dominated by a group of composers who continued to apply the late-Romantic tendencies, enriching them with the moderate use of modern forms of expression as well as intonations of folk music. The leading figure was Juozas Gruodis, the founder of the Lithuanian professional school of composition and of the Kaunas Conservatoire. His work (as well as that of his contemporaries and followers, Vladas Jakubėnas and Kazimieras Viktoras Banaitis, who both subsequently emigrated to the USA) amalgamated Romantic, Expressionist and Impressionist musical language with the qualities of folk songs, aiming at creating a folklore-based national musical style.

Simultaneously, a more radical and modernist-oriented group of composers emerged: Vytautas Bacevičius, Jeronimas Kačinskas, and Julius Gaidelis (all of them fled to the USA during the Second World War). The work of Bacevičius (seven symphonies, music and piano concertos) is marked with elements of Constructivism and Expressionism; his music is atonal and athemic. During the late period of his work, Bacevičius, under the influence of Hindu philosophy, worked on the creation of "cosmic music," in his own language (*Cosmic Poem* for piano, *Cosmic Rays* for organ).

The Second World War and the subsequent Soviet occupation interrupted the natural development of Lithuanian music. Art became subject to the compulsory Socialist Realism (progressive contents, using popular means of expression). As for music, this resulted in the application of an extremely traditional (19th-century Romantic-style) musical language: pompous epic, the almost obligatory "from darkness to light" model of symphonic cycles, which were to end with "popular celebration", and finally the excessive use of folk song melodies.

The Warsaw Autumn festivals of modern music that took place in neighbouring Poland served as a window to the world for Lithuanian music. Lithuanian composers originally attended these festivals as observers, but later as full participants. The Warsaw festivals allowed the phenomena of 20th-century music – atonality, dodecaphony, sonoristic, aleatoric, and the collage technique – to enter Lithuanian music.

The revolution in musical language at the beginning of the 1960s was started by the composers of the older generation: Eduardas Balsys, whose works were strongly marked by expressionist features, and Julius Juzeliūnas, whose work was more neo-Classical. This tendency was subsequently continued by the younger composers (Vytautas Barkauskas, Vytautas Montvila, etc.), whereas the most radical innovator was Antanas Rekašius, who used aleatoric means widely, as well as parody and grotesque. Leading musical pieces of that period include Juzeliūnas' *African Sketches*, Balsys' *Don't Touch the Blue Globe* and *Dramatic Frescoes*, Barkauskas' *Poetry*, *Intimate Composition* and *Pro Memoria* and Rekašius' symphonies.

Another stage in the development of Lithuanian music was reached in 1970 when the search for an individual style and non-traditional genres increased markedly. The conflict dramaturgy of music was diminishing. Instead, pieces for chamber groups became increasingly popular. As a reaction against the music of Expressionist hypertrophy and texture satiation, the influence of Minimalism, new simplicity (New Romanticism) and similar trends became visible. The works of Feliksas Bajoras, Bronius Kutavičius and Osvaldas Balakauskas earned wide recognition in Lithuania and abroad.

In many instances, Kutavičius relies on the fundamental impulses of folk music; his pieces are marked with a unique treatment of time and space. This composer is considered the pioneer of Minimalism in Lithuanian music. His oratorios *The Last Pagan Rites*, *Out Of the Jotvingiai Stone* and *Magic Wheel of Sanskrit* are very theatrical, like reconstructions of ancient folk rituals or pagan rites. Through non-classical and non-academic means,

Kutavičius creates a new professional national art. Highlighting the folklore or even pre-folklore and pantheistic elements in his music, he reconstructs from surviving fragments the formerly indivisible and integral unity of national culture.

Although Bajoras' music is referred to as the New Folklorism, it is far from being just a reconstruction or stylisation of folk

music. For him, music can amalgamate the folklore mentality and late 20th-century forms of expression. In his works, a number of musical worlds are present simultaneously: neo-Romanticism, Expressionism, neo-Classicism, Lithuanian folk music, serial techniques, sonoristics, and sometimes hints of popular music. Some aspects of Bajoras' opera *Lamb of God* could be of importance even to world opera of the late 20th century.

Balakauskas is one of the few Lithuanian composers who has created his own precise and unique system of musical language (harmony and rhythmics). He refers to it as dodecaphony. Balakauskas' system is related to the musical theories of Hindemith (the argument of the acoustic relatedness of sounds) and Messiaen (symmetrical mode and rhythmic structures).

In the 1980s, the New Romanticists appeared. This tendency is represented first of all by Algirdas Martinaitis, Mindaugas Urbaitis, Vidmantas Bartulis and Onutė Narbutaitė. They feature literary and neo-Romantic ideas, the stylistics of chamber minimalism which are manifested in archaic

THE NATIONAL SYMPHONY ORCHESTRA

211

folk music features, diatonics, the simplicity of rhythm and melody.

Martinaitis' works are strongly marked with a feeling for nature and ethnicity (*Music of the Last Gardens* for oboe, piano, cello and drums, *Keyboard of Live Water* for two pianos and synthesiser, etc.).

Urbaitis is considered to be a leading Lithuanian Minimalist. However, his minimalism is of a different nature from Kutavičius'. It is more radical and more closely related to world trends in minimalist music. His work is explicitly rational and is marked by the quest for clarity of style, integrity of the piece, and artistic purity.

Bartulis' music is characterised by a natural, rather slow but constant flow. The leading motif is repeated, interpreted and developed until it attains a specific stage in its structure and leads to a new musical and dramatic stage. The masses of sounds or stylised episodes appear dramatically, they are written in differing and closed form (viz., fugue); quotations from the music of the past are also used (Chopin, Brahms, Beethoven, Bach). Bartulis received the National Prize in 1998 for his *Concerto for Piano and Orchestra*, the opera *Lesson* and the string quartet *Oh Darling*.

Narbutaitė's music can be described as intellectual lyrics, which utilise numerous associations with literature and the fine arts. Her piece *Opuslugubre* for string orchestra is related to the tragic events of 13 January 1991 in Lithuania, and reaches suggestive heights. She also wrote *Simfonia col triangolo* for chamber orchestra. Her oratorio *Centones meae urbi* earned her the National Prize in 1997.

The main centres for performing professional music are the National Philharmonic Hall,

THE BAROQUE PAŽAISLIS MONASTERY (EARLY 18TH CENTURY) IN KAUNAS HOSTS REGULAR MUSIC FESTIVALS

the National Opera and Ballet Theatre, the Kaunas State Musical Theatre and Klaipėda Musical Theatre. Since 1997, the Philharmonic Hall has hosted the annual international Vilnius Festival from May to July. The Pažaislis Music Festival, held amid the Baroque splendour of the Pažaislis Monastery outside Kaunas, lasts the whole summer.

Since 1991, the Festival of Young Musicians has taken place in Kaunas. Participants in it are children under 16, many of them winners of international competitions. They are offered courses under the Ars Baltica programme. Also, the Philharmonic Hall regularly hosts international quartet festivals and concert weeks devoted to famous composers.

International recognition has been earned by the Lithuanian Chamber Orchestra (led by Professor Saulius Sondeckis), the Lithuanian State Symphony Orchestra (conducted by Gintaras Rinkevičius), the Lietuva State Ensemble of Songs and Dances, the Trimitas Lithuanian State Brass Orchestra, the Vilnius and Čiurlionis quartets, and other groups.

Many individual performers, like the opera singers Virgilijus Noreika and Irena Milkevičiūtė, and the ballet dancer Eglė Špo-

kaitė, have devotees in Lithuania and abroad. Mūza Rubackytė, a professor at the European Conservatoire in Paris, has won numerous international piano competitions. Other internationally acclaimed musicians are the pianist Petras Geniušas, the piano duo of Rūta and Zbignevas Ibelhauptas, and the violinists Raimundas Katilius and the young Vilhelmas Čepinskis.

Students are trained for music and theatre careers at the Music Academy in Vilnius, which also has branches in Kaunas and Klaipėda. Almost 10,000 students have graduated from the academy since it opened its doors. Ballet is taught at the Vilnius Ballet School.

ARCHITECTURE

The earliest examples of Lithuanian architecture are over 700 fortified hills, which are protected as archaeological monuments. The oldest surviving stone construction is the late 13th-century ruin of Medininkai Castle, located about 20 miles east of Vilnius. It is currently undergoing restoration.

Gothic architecture started spreading across Lithuania in the 14th century. Throughout the next century the style dominated in the building of castles, churches and houses. In the early castles, for instance in Trakai, traditional Baltic and Gothic ways of using bricks were used together, as well as Gothic forms for the windows. The best surviving examples include Trakai Castle (located 30km southwest of Vilnius); St Anne's, and the Bernadine Church in Vilnius; St George's, and the Vytautas Church, with their monasteries, and the Perkūnas House, in Kaunas.

Renaissance architecture in Lithuania in the 16th and 17th centuries was strongly influenced by architects from Italy and the Netherlands. The Italian architects Bernardo Zanobi da Gianoti and Giovani Cini, and the Dutch architects Peter Nonhaart and J. van Laer worked in Lithuania. Among the best pieces of Renaissance architecture are St Michael's Church, the Gates of Dawn, and the Lower Castle (destroyed in 1800, its foundations are currently being excavated by archaeologists) in Vilnius; the Trinitarian and Lutheran churches in Kaunas; and St Peter and Paul's Church in Šiauliai. The most notable example of military architecture from the period is

A BAROQUE MASTERPIECE IN VILNIUS: ST PETER AND PAUL'S CHURCH CONTAINS OVER 2,000 DIFFERENT SCULPTURES

Biržai Castle and Palace. About this time the buildings of Vilnius University were begun.

Baroque architecture appeared at the beginning of the 17th century. The first buildings in this style were designed by Italian archi-tects. Later, the local Vilnius Baroque school emerged. The construction of many churches, monasteries and palaces was undertaken: the churches of St Peter and Paul, St Casimir and St Theresa were built in Vilnius.

Architects of the Vilnius Baroque school created the Missionaries', St Johns' and other churches. Pažaislis church, near Kaunas, and many palaces were constructed during the period of mature Baroque. Like most Baroque architecture, these churches are marked by their dynamic forms and complex altarpieces, heavily decorated with flowing ornamentation.

During the Classical revival architectural links were deepened

THE SMUGLEVIČIUS HALL HOLDS THE RAREST VOLUMES IN VILNIUS UNIVERSITY LIBRARY. THE LIBRARY HAS A RICH COLLECTION OF 15TH TO 18TH-CENTURY PUBLICATIONS.

with St Petersburg, Warsaw and France. The most distinguished exponent of Lithuanian Classicism was Laurynas Stuoka-Gucevičius, the first head of the Architecture Department at Vilnius University, who designed Vilnius Cathedral, an architectural masterpiece. Other well-known architects who worked at that time were Martynas Knakfusas (Knackfuss) and Karolis Podčašinskis. The Town Hall and the Governor General's Palace (now the President's Office) were built in Vilnius, as well as the Tyszkiewicz palace and other estates in the provinces.

The most notable pieces of inter-war architecture are in Kaunas, which at that time was the interim capital. Some buildings continued the neo-Classical tradition (the Bank of Lithuania); others (the milk processing plant, the General Post Office, gymnasiums, and many houses) were marked with a quest for rationality and functionality. During the period of independence, the Vytautas Magnus cultural complex (today the Museum of War and the M.K. Čiurlionis Art Museum) and the clinic complex, formerly the largest in the Baltic states, were built. Leading architects of that time were Mykolas Songaila, Vladimiras Dubeneckis

and Vytautas Landsbergis-Žemkalnis.

The Soviet era was marked by the construction of industrial, office and housing complexes, which were distinguished by their functionalism as well as uniformity. One of the best known examples of late Soviet architecture is the Vilnius Opera and Ballet Theatre.

The potential and activity of today's architects were well demonstrated by the projects in the Lithuanian Expo 2000 pavilion in Hanover in 1998. With the assistance of the Canadian Institute of Urban Studies, a general plan for Vilnius has been prepared.

Lithuania's architectural heritage consists of over a thousand sets of buildings or single objects classified as cultural treasures, as well as over 70 settlements, small towns or historic parts of cities. UNESCO declared the centre of Vilnius – its Old Town – a World Heritage Site in 1994. The third regeneration project for this part of the town was prepared in 1992; the strategy for its revival, with the assistance of the World Bank, was finalised in 1996. Considerable renovation work in the Old Town was carried out in 1998. Archaeological research in the Lower Castle, and plans for its rebuilding, are also under way.

Churches are being restored and renovated, as are the old quarters of other towns and cities. With UNESCO's support, Lithuania became a co-ordination centre for training on the preservation of the cultural heritage for the Baltic states, Belarus and Ukraine.

FOLK MUSIC AND ART

Lithuanian folk art and musical traditions include *sutartinė* (round) singing, family musical activities, pan-pipes, the songs of deportees and partisans, chants, traditions and rites of marriage, agricultural ceremonies, playing the *kanklės* (a sort of zither), as well as trade-related holidays and festivities. The richness of the Lithuanian folk music heritage can be appreciated by the following: the Institute of Lithuanian Literature and Folklore has catalogued over 500,000 distinct folk songs.

Vilnius becomes a colourful place during the Kaziukas Fair on 4 March, the day of St Casimir, the patron saint of Lithuania. This crafts tradition has continued since the end of the 19th century. In 1971 the first Potters' Day was held, which triggered national days of various other crafts: metal working, weaving and wood carving. Craftsmen compete and exhibit their work; a holiday atmosphere is also created by folk singing and dancing.

During the post-war years, a multitude of folk-music ensembles appeared. They are assisted by 967 cultural centres, employing almost 3,000 music specialists, performers, choir leaders and ethnomusicologists. They are trained at Klaipėda University, Vilnius Music Academy, and five conservatoires. Lithuania has 4,328 amateur folk groups. On average, they hold about 65,000 concerts and evenings annually.

Song festivals have been held since 1924. The most popular song festival occurred in 1985, attracting 38,856 participants. World Lithuanian Song Festivals are attended by emigrants from Canada, the USA, Australia, Germany, Argentina and Russia.

Lithuania has 2,163 choirs and vocal groups, which include over 42,000 singers; 753 orchestras and instrumental groups, with 8,000 musicians; 1,854 dance groups, with over 30,000 dancers; 1,571 amateur theatre groups, with 24,000 actors; 828 folklore groups, with almost 13,000 members. In all almost 130,000 people participate in folklore performances.

PUBLIC INSTITUTIONS, MUSEUMS

The Constitution of the Republic of Lithuania guarantees the right to form societies, political parties and associations, provided that their aims and activities do not contravene the Constitution or the law.

NON-GOVERNMENTAL ORGANISATIONS

Examples of non-governmental organisations are public organisations, associations and foundations, most non-profit organisations, trade unions, religious and ethnic communities, residents' associations, etc. They can be founded by anybody who has reached the age of 18. Non-governmental organisations are regulated by the laws on public organisations, associations, charities and support foundations.

The Non-Governmental Organisations Information and Support Centre was established in 1995. Its main activity is supplying information to Lithuanian and other organisations and international assistance institutions, and also consulting and training. Lithuania has over 5,000 non-governmental organisations.

RELIGIONS

The Constitution does not make provision for a state religion. The 1995 Law on Religious Societies and Communities confirmed nine religious groups which are recognised by the state: Roman Catholics, Catholics of Eastern Rites (Uniates), the Orthodox Church, Old Believers, Evangelical Reformers, Evangelical Lutherans, Jews, Karaites, and Sunni Muslims. These communities have been in Lithuania for over 300 years.

The law includes provisions on the procedure for religious communities to obtain state recognition. This may be awarded by the Seimas if the religious community is formally registered and has been in Lithuania for at least

25 years, has public support, and has been sufficiently integrated into society and the cultural heritage. Religious communities recognised by the state enjoy legal status and may provide instruction in their faith at state educational institutions.

According to sociological data, 60% to 80% of Lithuania's inhabitants consider themselves Roman Catholics. The Roman Catholic Church began taking root in the 14th century, approximately at the same time that the Jewish, Karaite and Tartar religious traditions appeared in the Grand Duchy of Lithuania. Protestants first became active in Lithuania in the 16th century; they were joined by Old Believers in the 17th century. The Orthodox tradition has been present since the 13th century.

The most numerous non-traditional religious community in Lithuania is the New Apostolic Church. The first communities appeared in the first half of the 20th century but were eradicated during the Soviet occupation. They were re-established in 1991 and currently have about 5,000 members. Other relatively numerous religious communities include Baptists, Pentecostalists and Seventh Day Adventists.

There are also quasi-Christian groups, which include Jehova's Witnesses and Mormons. The oldest group of Oriental origin is the Krishna Consciousness Organisation. There are also cults, including the Baha'i movement and the Unification Church. Recently, neo-pagan groups have started emerging, with the Romuva group being perhaps the best known. Lastly, there are psychocults, including the Harmony Consultancy Company of Socionics and the Vilnius Academy of Parapsychology.

POLITICAL PARTIES

A political party or organisation is required to have at least 400 members to be officially registered. Political parties are regulated by the Law on Political Parties and Political Organisations. By the beginning of 1999, the Ministry of Justice had registered 35 political parties and organisations. The major ones include the Homeland Union (Lithuanian Conservatives), the Centrist Union, the Christian Democratic Party, the Lithuanian Democratic Labour Party, the Social Democratic Party and the Liberal Union.

MASS MEDIA

In 1999 there were 25 radio stations transmitting regular programmes in Lithuania. Three state-owned and five private radio stations can be heard across the whole of the country. Of the latter, the radio station M-1 was the first independent, commercial radio station in Central and Eastern Europe. It began broadcasting in 1989.

Almost the entire population has access to four TV stations: Lithuanian National Television and three private broadcasters (LNK, TV-3 and Baltic Television).

There are eight regional TV stations. About 60 licences for operating cable TV have been issued.

A total of 263 magazines and 439 newspapers are published in Lithuania. Their circulation amounts to over 2.7 million copies.

Magazines and newspapers are issued in Lithuanian, English, Russian, Polish, German and other languages.

The largest daily, *Lietuvos rytas*, has a circulation of 64,000 (the circulation of the Saturday edition is over 223,000). *Respublika, Lietuvos aidas, Kauno diena* and *Lietuvos žinios* are the other widely read dailies.

TRADITIONAL INTERNATIONAL FESTIVALS

Sartai horse race on ice (first Saturday of February)

Festival of Young Musicians in Kaunas (April)

Cinema Spring (April) Vilnius 2000 (eclectic, May-December)

In Vogue Fashion Festival (May)

Poetry Spring (end of May)

Vilnius Festival (music, May-July)

Skamba skamba kankliai Folklore Festival (end of May)

Pažaislis Music Festival (June-August)

Trakai Music Festival (July-August)

Klaipėda Sea Festival (end of July)

Vilnius Days Street Festival (August)

M.K.Čiurlionis Piano and Organ Competition (September)

Autumn Theatre Forum (October)

Vilnius Jazz Festival (October)

HOLIDAYS

1 January – New Year
16 February – Lithuanian Independence Day (1918)
11 March – Restoration of Independence (1990)
Easter Sunday and Monday
1st Sunday of May – Mother's Day
6 July – Coronation of Mindaugas, King of Lithuania
1 November – All Saints
25–26 December – Christmas

ART GALLERIES AND MUSEUMS

Lithuania has 85 museums, including three national, 16 state, 52 regional, 12 departmental and two private ones. National and state museums hold collections and exhibitions of archaeology, history and folk art. Regional museums are chiefly folk or commemorative.

The first museum in Lithuania was quite unusual: it was established in 1812 in the trunk of a huge hollowed-out oak tree. The writer Dionizas Poška, its founder, collected and exhibited historical relics, thus stimulating interest in the nation's past and resistance to increasing Russification. This museum still exists.

In 1855, the Museum of Antiquities was established in Vilnius and evolved into today's Lithuanian National Museum. The first state museum, the Vytautas Magnus Cultural Museum in Kaunas, was established in the 1920s.

Lithuania's museums attract over two million visitors annually. They contain over three million art and historical exhibits.

National Gallery

Although the National Gallery is located outside the historic centre of Vilnius, it is still worth visiting. A permanent display of folk sculpture, painting, furniture and linen is shown in stark, modernist surroundings. Lithuanian art of the early 20th century is also shown here, as are occasional exhibitions.

The building is as interesting as its contents, being arranged as a group of boxes on different levels, joined by a series of staircases and mezzanines. One window the length of the wall gives a sweeping view of the city and the Neris.

Vilnius Picture Gallery

Lithuanian art is given its fullest showing in the Vilnius Picture Gallery. Here, in a former nobleman's palace, all the main movements from the 16th to the end of the 19th century are represented. This includes Baroque, Classical and Romantic painting. Several rooms are devoted to the architect Laurynas Stuoka-Gucevičius, and to the painter Pranciskus Smuglevičius, who both worked in the Classical style and collaborated on the design of Vilnius Cathedral.

The palace's rooms have recently been restored and are occasionally used as a venue for chamber music concerts.

M.K. Čiurlionis Art Museum

Also in Kaunas is the M.K. Čiurlionis Art Museum, which houses the largest single collection of work by the turn-of-the- century composer and artist Mikalojus Konstantinas Čiurlionis, and where visitors may listen to recordings of his music. In addition, this gallery shows 20th-century Lithuanian painting and sculpture, and Lithuanian folk art.

Radvila Palace Museum

Another gallery in the Old Town in Vilnius is the Radvila Palace, housing an extensive collection of European art. It includes paintings by Salvator Rosa, Hobbema and Jacob van Ruisdale, and prints by Piranesi, Canaletto, Durer, Rembrandt and Goya.

The collection covers the development of European art, from the Italian Renaissance to the early 20th century.

It has its origins in the exhibitions held in the first half of the present century when privately owned works were shown to the public. Some were then donated to the Lithuanian Art Society, which began to build up an art collection. It was later supplemented after the Second World War with works confiscated from pivate collections and the church by the Soviet authorities.

Art enthusiasts will find the Radvila Palace a delight. They will be impressed by the range and quality of the collection, and by its display in pleasant, well-proportioned rooms.

The M. Žilinskas Gallery

The M. Žilinskas Gallery in Kaunas is also a modern, purpose-built gallery with another very impressive collection of art. Though not as comprehensive as the Radvila Palace in Vilnius, it is larger and covers certain schools extremely well.

One room is devoted to ancient art, mainly from Egypt, including two mummies, and also Greek and Roman amphorae and other artefacts. Other rooms hold Italian, French, Flemish and

Dutch paintings, including a painting by Rubens. In addition to works by Corot, Courbet, Manet and Renoir, the gallery holds a large number of turn-of-the-century German paintings. An extensive section on applied art includes porcelain, tapestries and furniture from Europe, Russia and the Far East.

The Rumšiškės Open-Air Museum of Country Life

The country's history is told in a number of large and small museums. The Open-Air Museum of Country Life at Rumšiškės covers 175 hectares and contains around 150 buildings from different regions and periods. There are houses, farms, windmills, several villages and even a small town. Most of the buildings are authentic, having been physically transplanted from their original sites; some are replicas, being built especially for the museum. It occupies a varied landscape on the shores of a man-made lake beside the main Vilnius-Kaunas motorway. The museum is about 70km from Vilnius.

Lithuanian History Museums

The Trakai Historical Museum is situated in the dramatic castle on an island in Lake Galvė. It cov-

ers the history of Lithuania during its "Golden Age" in the Middle Ages and illustrates it with weapons and other artefacts. A museum in another part of the castle holds an impressive collection of silver, porcelain and other objects of applied art.

In Vilnius, the Lithuanian National Museum and Gediminas Castle, both devoted to the country's history, are situated at the heart of the city.

These are just a few of the many history museums across the country. Every major town, and many smaller ones, have museums about the past. Many regions have their own outdoor museums.

Amber

In addition, there is a large number of museums devoted to special subjects. The biggest specialised amber museum in the world was founded in Palanga 34 years ago. The museum covers an area of 700 square metres, and in its rooms on two floors about 4,500 exhibits are on display. In its vaults the museum has a further 28,000 exhibits. It has already been visited by more than 7.5 million people.

The whole history of amber, from its formation to its possible applications, is displayed in the museum's showcases. In the archaeology rooms findings from the Stone Age and later times, which were excavated during archaeological expeditions all over Lithuania, are on display.

Visitors spend most of their time looking through magnifying glasses at the illuminated prehistoric plants, seeds and insects caught in resin some 50 million years ago.

On the ground floor, against a dark blue and claret background, works in amber of Lithuanian craftsmen are arranged. There is one room in which the exhibition is changed each year so that every artist can show his skill. Formerly this room was the palace chapel.

The palace was built in the Neo-Renaissance style in 1897 and belonged to the large and famous Tiškevičius family which contributed greatly to the development of Lithuanian culture. They lived in Palanga and were not only the first professional archaeologists in the country (in 1855 they founded a museum of antiquities in Vilnius), but also large-scale collectors of works of art.

It was after Count Tiškevičius bought an estate in Palanga that the town became famous as a resort. Through his efforts a school and the first hospital in Lithuania were established, and the first Lithuanian play was performed in Palanga. He was the main sponsor when the church was built, and the bricks used for its construction were made at his brickyard.

The count's collection of archaeological amber is now at the museum. After the Soviets occupied Lithuania the family emigrated and the palace and the huge park were nationalised.

Devils

This is a museum that grew out of a private collection. A local artist called Antanas Žmuidzinavičius began to collect figures of devils in 1906. Shortly after his death 60 years later at the age of 90, the devils were put on public display in his house in Kaunas.

However, the collection continued to grow and a two-storey extension was built to accommodate the gifts. At present there are about 3,000 different pieces.

Why collect devils? In the words of the collection's founder: "The devil is a symbol of the dark. Without the dark it would be impossible to see the light. The more devils, the more distinct the light."

Folk Instruments

Beginning with wooden pipes, whistles made from reeds and

horns made from rolled birch bark, and ending with modern accordions, the Folk Instrument Museum in Kaunas shows the evolution of folk instruments.

A whole room is dedicated to *kanklės,* a sort of zither. Curiosities include a set of bagpipes, and a bladder bass - a stringed instrument like a cello, using an animal bladder for amplification. The last of the eight rooms shows accordions, harmoniums and concertinas.

Although the emphasis is on Lithuanian folk music, the collection includes many instruments from other countries.

History of Medicine

The Museum of Medicine and Pharmacy in Kaunas begins with a display of lucky talismans and explores its subject through recreations of doctor's and dentist's examining rooms, a hospital ward and a complete chemist's shop with wooden cabinets, a counter and till, and jars of medicine. Low doorways and a tortuous staircase lead down to the basement of this handsome house in Kaunas. Here in the vaulted cellars are displayed lucky talismans and early medicines.

In the more spacious upstairs rooms are pieces of equipment for preparing medicines.

Clocks

In Klaipėda, the Clock Museum shows the history of timekeeping, from early sundials to electronic clocks, and is set in the house of a wealthy merchant who used to live in Klaipėda at the beginning of the 19th century.

The museum explains not only the mechanisms but also the development of clock design. It is worth lingering in the museum's elegant rooms when the hour is struck to hear the chorus of assorted chimes.

Bicycles

The presence of a bicycle factory in Šiauliai explains why the city has a bicycle museum. It shows the development of bicycles from 1905 to the present day. The exhibition includes two-seater tricycles, tandems and exercise bicycles, also pumps, baggage carriers, lights, reflectors and dynamos.

Lithuanian-made bicycles are on display too, from older models, with names such as Vyturėlis (Skylark), Kregždutė (Swallow) and Ereliukas (Eaglet), to the recent models Niagara, Jumpman and Terminator.

The Maironis Museum of Lithuanian Literature

This museum is located in the Old Town of Kaunas near the Town

Hall. The building in which the Maironis museum is housed was built in the Baroque style and served as the residence of a wealthy town dweller. Jonas Mačiulis-Maironis, one of Lithuania's greatest poets, purchased this residence in 1909 and lived in it until his death in 1932.

The Maironis museum was established in 1936. At first the museum included three rooms of the Maironis residence. In 1941, the museum began accumulating exhibits of other Lithuanian writers as well. Gradually it evolved into the equivalent of a national museum of literature.

At present the museum preserves 200,000 items and 600 collections of archival material, manuscripts, autographed books and personal belongings of Lithuanian writers. Beginning in 1989, the Maironis museum began receiving exhibits of Lithuanian exile writers.

THE FISHERMAN'S HOUSE MUSEUM IN NIDA

SPORTS

Sport, in the modern sense of the word, gained popularity after 1918 when the country declared independence. In 1919 the Sports Union was established; the National Olympic Committee was founded five years later. In 1924 Lithuanian sportsmen (a soccer team and two cyclists) participated for the first time in the Olympic Games in Paris, and subsequently in 1928 in the St Moritz Winter Olympic Games.

Lithuanian sportsmen won international recognition in the 1930s. In 1937 and 1939 the basketball team, with the help of American Lithuanian basketball players, won the European championship. From this time on basketball was established as something akin to the national sport of Lithuania.

After the Second World War, Lithuanian basketball players were often among the stars of Soviet basketball. Steponas Bu-

THE UTENA RACETRACK (EASTERN LITHUANIA)

tautas, Justinas Lagunavičius and Kazys Petkevičius, playing on the Soviet team, brought back the first silver medals from the Helsinki Olympics. Later, numerous players were awarded gold medals: Modestas Paulauskas in 1972; Angelė Rupšienė in 1976 and 1980; and Valdemaras Chomičius, Rimas Kurtinaitis, Šarūnas Marčiulionis and Arvydas Sabonis in 1988 in Seoul.

After regaining independence in 1990, the national basketball team participated in the Barcelona and Atlanta Olympics, winning bronze medals. The Kaunas Žalgiris basketball team won the Intercontinental R.V. Jones Cup in 1986 and the European Basketball Cup in 1998, due particularly to the tireless efforts of their coaches, Vladas Garastas and Jonas Kazlauskas.

Women are equally active in basketball. In 1938 in Rome they came second in Europe, and in 1997 they won the European championship in Budapest.

Lithuania's cyclists were successful in the Seoul Olympics: Gintautas Umaras brought home two gold medals. In women's cycling in 1998, Diana Žiliūtė became world champion, and Edita Pučinskaite won the prestigious Tour de France. Laima Zilporytė and Rasa and Jolanta Polike-

DIANA ŽILIŪTĖ, WORLD CHAMPION, VALKEMBOURG, 1998

vičiūtė have also joined the ranks of the most promising cyclists in the world. They were trained by Narsutis Dumbauskas, Viktoras Konovalovas, and others.

Lithuania is becoming well known thanks to its sport dancers. The Klaipėda Žuvėdra sport dancing group has competed successfully in Europe. Equally well known are Donatas Vėželis and Lina Chatkevičiūtė, winners of the 1998 World Youth Competition, and their trainers Jūratė and Česlovas Norvaiša.

Lithuania's first Olympic champion was the boxer Danas Pozniakas (1968 Mexico); the first track-and-field athletics champion of independent Lithuania

ARVYDAS SABONIS

was Romas Ubartas (1992 Barcelona), whose endeavours are continued by Virgilijus Alekna, a gifted discus thrower. Over 250 Olympics participants have won 26 gold, 19 silver and 39 bronze medals.

The country's achievements have also been supplemented by individual athletes. Vilhelmina Bardauskienė was the first woman in the world to jump over seven metres. The mountaineer Vladas Vitkauskas climbed the highest peaks and raised the flag of Lithuania on every continent between 1993 and 1996. Vidmantas Urbonas, a triathlete and five-times world vice-champion, won two cups in Mexico in 1998 in the tenfold ultra-triathlon (swimming 76km, cycling 3,600km and running 840km). Piotras Silkinas of Kretinga is a champion in the 1,000-mile marathon. The pilot Jurgis Kairys became a world vice-champion in high altitude flying.

Sports competition today is a highly organised undertaking, which nevertheless draws support from a variety of private and official sources, including individuals, companies, banks and the Government. Some of the most successful handball, football and basketball teams are financed by and represent private enterprises, which view this assistance as a form of marketing. This mixed arrangement evolved gradually from the last years of Soviet rule when sports, as well as many other spheres of life, were still subject to rigid, central government control. Decentralisation of the management of sports paralleled other moves towards liberalisation and decontrol in governance, culture and the economy. A key event (significant for both sports and the country as a whole) was the establishment of the National Olympic Committee on 11 December 1988. The Olympic Academy was established in 1989, and the par-Olympic Committee in 1990. Today there are almost 100 federations, unions and associations of various sports branches.

VLADAS VITKAUSKAS ON MOUNT EVEREST, 1993

233

HOW TO REACH
LITHUANIA

Visa requirements

Visa requirements are being eliminated at a steady rate, and currently citizens of all Western European countries as well as of the USA, Canada, Australia, Japan and Korea do not require visas for travel to Lithuania. The same applies to most Central and Eastern European countries, with some exceptions.

In other cases, Lithuanian consular authorities issue the following kinds of visas: diplomatic, official, regular, special and transit. Diplomatic and official visas are issued to foreign citizens enjoying diplomatic privileges and other privileges who travel on official business to Lithuania. Regular visas are issued to foreign persons travelling to visit acquaintances, for tourism or other similar purposes. Regular visas are valid for a year. The total length of stay in Lithuania with a regular visa may not exceed 90 days a year from the first day of arrival in Lithuania.

The following list, provided by the Lithuanian Ministry of Foreign Affairs, includes those countries whose citizens do not need visas as of July, 1999:

Australia	Denmark	Japan	Slovakia
Austria	Estonia	Korea	Slovenia
Belarus*	Finland	Latvia	Spain
Belgium	France	Liechtenstein	Sweden
Bulgaria	Germany	Luxembourg	Switzerland
Canada	Greece	Malta	Turkey***
Chile****	Hungary	The Netherlands	Ukraine**
China **	Iceland	Norway	The United Kingdom
Croatia	Ireland	Poland	The United States of America
Cyprus	Israel**	Portugal	The Vatican
The Czech Republic	Italy	Romania**	Venezuela

* For holders of diplomatic passports only
** For holders of diplomatic and official passports only
*** For holders of diplomatic, official and special passports only
**** For holders of tourist passports only

234

CUSTOMS

Travellers arriving in Lithuania for a period not exceeding three days must have not less than 300 litas (75 USD) in cash or a corresponding amount in foreign currency. Those arriving for a period exceeding three days must have a minimum of 100 litas (25 USD) for each day of their planned stay, or a corresponding amount in foreign currency. This requirement does not apply to transit travellers, and to individuals coming for the purpose of studying, medical treatment and work upon their presentation of a certificate issued by the Ministry of the Interior.

BY AIR

The easiest way of travelling to Lithuania is by scheduled flights by Lithuanian Airlines or other carriers. There is a regular direct service between Vilnius and the following cities: Amsterdam, Berlin, Copenhagen, Frankfurt am Main, Helsinki, Istanbul, Kiev, London, Minsk, Moscow, Paris, Riga, Rome, Stockholm, Tallinn, Vienna and Warsaw. Additional air links are provided by LAL and several smaller carriers from Kaunas and Palanga to Scandinavian, German and Central European destinations.

BY FERRY

Sea ferries from Kiel (Germany), Ahus (Sweden), Stockholm, Mukran (Germany), Copenhagen, Fredericia (Denmark) and Aabendraa (Denmark) bring an average of 80,000 passengers to the port of Klaipeda each year.

INTERNET LINKS

A growing volume of current information about Lithuania is now available on a variety of Internet links. The following will help provide access to many official and private sources of information:

THE PRESIDENT OF THE REPUBLIC OF LITHUANIA
www.president.lt

THE SEIMAS (PARLIAMENT) OF THE REPUBLIC OF LITHUANIA
www.lrs.lt

THE GOVERNMENT OF THE REPUBLIC OF LITHUANIA
www.lrvk.lt

THE MINISTRY OF FOREIGN AFFAIRS
www.urm.lt

THE EUROPEAN COMMITTEE UNDER THE GOVERNMENT OF LITHUANIA
www.euro.lt

LITHUANIAN DEVELOPMENT AGENCY
www.lda.lt

THE TOURISM DEPARTMENT
www.tourism.lt

MAIN LITHUANIAN INTERNET RESOURCES
www.online.lt   neris.mii.lt
www.search.lt

VILNIUS IN YOUR POCKET, TOURIST GUIDE TO VILNIUS, KAUNAS AND KLAIPĖDA
PUBLISHED QUARTERLY
www.inyourpocket.com

UDK 908(474.5)
Li 578

Texts written by:
IRENA ALEKSAITĖ, ALGIS AVIŽIENIS, ALFREDAS BUMBLAUSKAS,
DAVID BURGESS, PETRAS BRAŽĖNAS, GIEDRIUS DRUKTEINIS,
JOSEPH EVERATT, BIRUTĖ GARBARAVIČIENĖ, JONAS GLEMŽA,
ALIJUŠAS GRĖBLIŪNAS, PAVEL LAVRINEC, JŪRATĖ MARKEVIČIENĖ,
SELEMONAS PALTANAVIČIUS, LINAS PAULAUSKIS, NATALIJA PAULINKIENĖ,
ARŪNAS PEČKAITIS, LEONAS PELECKIS-KAKTAVIČIUS,
JURGITA PETRONYTĖ, VYTAUTAS PURONAS, VIDA RIMEIKIENĖ,
JAN SAVICKI, ERIKAS SLAVĖNAS, ALGIMANTAS SLIVINSKAS,
ALEKSANDRAS ŠIDLAUSKAS, VITAS ŪSAS, ARVYDAS VALIONIS,
DANUTĖ ZOVIENĖ, JONAS ŽILINSKAS

Photography by:
JONAS AMBRAŠKA, STANISLOVAS BAGDONAVIČIUS, ARŪNAS BALTĖNAS,
JUOZAS BALTIEJUS, ROMUALDAS BARAUSKAS, DŽOJA GUNDA BARYSAITĖ,
LAIMIS BRUNDZA, VITALIJUS BUTYRINAS, RIČARDAS DAILIDĖ,
VLADIMIRAS GULEVIČIUS (ELTA), MINDAUGAS KULBIS (LIETUVOS
RYTAS), GINTARAS MAČIULIS, VALDAS MALINAUSKAS,
DMITRIJ MATVEJEV, DENIS NANDE, ZENONAS NEKROŠIUS,
SELEMONAS PALTANAVIČIUS, SIGITAS JONAS PLATŪKIS, ALFREDAS PLIADIS,
ROMUALDAS POŽERSKIS, ALGIRDAS RAKAUSKAS, VIRGILIJUSUSINAVIČIUS,
VACYS VALUŽIS, KĘSTUTIS VANAGAS (ELTA), AUDRIUS ZAVADSKIS,
ALGIMANTAS ŽIŽIŪNAS,
"LITHUANIA IN THE WORLD" ARCHIVES
Art Director
ALGIMANTAS DAPŠYS

Printed by VILSPA, Lithuania

ISBN 9986-647-09-6

L

BALTIC SEA

● Skuodas   Mažeikiai ⬤   ◨ Naujoji
                                       Akmenė   ● Jonis

                    Platelių ež.

● Palanga   Telšiai ■   Kuršėnai ●
● Kretinga   ● Plungė   ◨ Šiauliai   ● Pak

                                                          ● Radvi
■ Klaipėda
  ● Gargždai   *Lūkstas*   ● Kelmė

KURŠIŲ LAGOON

Nemunas   ● Šilalė

Neringa   ● Šilutė   ● Raseiniai

                    Jūra   ● Kėda

                Tauragė ■   *Dubysa*

● Sovetsk   Jurbarkas ⬤   *Neručis*
                                        Nemunas

                                            ● Šakiai
            ⬤ Krasnoznamensk   Kauna
RUSSIA   Garliav

                                              Kazlų Rūda
● Černjachovsk   Kybartai ●   ● Pric
        ● Gusev   ● Vilkaviškis

                                        Marijampolė ■

                                            ● Kalvarija   *Vilyčionas*

                                              ● Lazdijai
POLAND

Suwałki ●

                                              ● Drusk

Augustów ●